ABC of Magic Charms

The Witches' Almanac, Ltd.
Publishers   Providence, Rhode Island

Address all inquiries and information to
THE WITCHES' ALMANAC, LTD.
P.O. Box 1292
Newport, RI 02840-9998

ISBN: 978-0-9773703-8-2

First Printing August 2009

Printed in Canada

FOREWORD

OBJECTS PROVIDING luck and protection surround us. Our challenge lies in recognizing them and availing ourselves of their power. Some, like High John the Conqueror Root or holed stones, are comparatively rare; others, like keys and knots, are easily obtainable. Exotic charms, like ankhs or engraved Gnostic gems, are clearly and obviously magical objects. Conversely, acorns, pine cones or kitchen herbs like basil, thyme and dill, are deceptively mundane: their innate magic powers easily overlooked. Lucky for us, Elizabeth Pepper has conjured and compiled *The ABC of Magic Charms*, a charming and extensive guide to power objects from around the world, from prehistoric times up until the present.

The category "magic charms" encompasses incantations (spoken charms) plus amulets, talismans and fetishes. All will be found within this book. The category "magic books" encompasses grimoires, books of shadows and spell books – but also almanacs. The occult history of almanacs is too often overlooked.

An almanac is a book, usually published annually and containing useful, practical information, such as moon phases, tide tables and weather predictions plus assorted wisdom and entertainment: poems, stories, recipes, factoids and miscellany. When almanacs first appeared in the fifteenth century, they were clearly and obviously books of magic; their intended audience those readers who sought to avail themselves of the wisdom of astrologers and seers.

Among the earliest publishers of almanacs were mystic masters like astrologer William Lilly, known as the "English Merlin" and Nostradamus whose still-controversial prophesies first appeared in the almanacs he wrote, compiled and published annually.

Over the centuries, however, as with so many other things (words, plants, animals and minerals for instance), the magical aspects of almanacs were de-emphasized and largely forgotten. Almanacs were relegated to the ranks of mundane reference materials, typically considered useful solely for readers seeking to farm, garden or fish.

When Elizabeth Pepper founded *The Witches' Almanac* in 1971 she revived the tradition of almanacs as magical books. Like her famous forebears, Pepper was an experienced and gifted practitioner of magic. *The Witches' Almanac* is suffused with the wisdom of the witch. In addition to the annual almanac, Pepper and *The Witches' Almanac* staff also compiled a number of excellent books on various magical subjects including *The ABC of Magic Charms*.

If you are new to *The Witches' Almanac* and its publications, I envy you. I remember very well the first time I encountered *The Witches' Almanac* and so I know first-hand what a wonderful journey you are about to commence. I was a teen-ager and I was immediately entranced by the charming and unpretentious little book jam-packed with magical information. If you are already familiar with *The Witches' Almanac*, then you recognize *The ABC of Magic Charms* as a valuable, reliable and entertaining old friend. This is a new, expanded version of the original text reflecting that, even after Pepper's death in 2005, a new edition of *The Witches' Almanac* appears each spring and continues to live up to Pepper's high standards. Lucky for us, Elizabeth Pepper amassed a brilliant and hard-working staff, dedicated to the age-old tradition of the magical book.

Judika Illes, author of *Pure Magic,*
Magic When You Need It,
The Encyclopedia of 5000 Spells,
The Element Encyclopedia of Witchcraft and
The Encyclopedia of Spirits

Primeval Garden   Antoine Vérard, Paris, 1506

FROM THE BEGINNING of time, an obscure quality within the human spirit has sought benefactions from the three kingdoms of Earth – animal, vegetable, mineral. Simple or complex, rare or commonplace, beautiful or awesome, all three share mysterious properties defined over the centuries by occult traditions. And it is from this bounty that we present a treasury of amulets, talismans, charms and fetishes – the symbols of mysticism and magic from prehistoric time to the present.

INTRODUCTION

THE WORDS charm, talisman, amulet, and fetish are often used interchangeably, although subtle distinctions exist.

Charm refers to an incantation, the verses sung over an object to imbue it with magical power, for the word derives from the Latin carmen, a song.

Talisman derives from either the Greek *telesma* or the Arabic *tilasm*, both of which connote a marked object over which a sacred rite has been performed. A talisman may be worn, carried, or just be present in the home, but it will have been consecrated for one specific purpose.

Amuletum in Latin means to baffle or do away with, and over time an amulet came to describe an ornament worn as a protective shield against evil.

The Portuguese word *feitiço* provides the English language with fetish, a natural object or carved image regarded as the dwelling place of a potent spiritual force. Originally it was applied to African religious artifacts by Christian colonists, for *feitiço* derives from the Latin *facticius*, artificial, or made by the sorcerer's art.

All practitioners of the hidden arts agree that a magic charm must first be purified, completely divested of any previous influence, before it can be consecrated. To release its innate power requires a ritual blessing which may be as elaborate as a prescribed dedication of ceremonial magic or as simple as traditional forms used by the shaman or witch. Ultimate success depends upon the power of the mind.

Ab: The ancient Egyptian ab or heart amulet represents the vitality and power of the subconscious mind. Although it came to be worn by the living, the ab was initially a funereal charm placed on the dead to signify the presence in the tomb of the living soul or spirit. This is based on the Egyptian belief that the heart was the source of life and thought and was considered to be the center of the soul. Always in shades of red, the usual ab resembles a stylized jug, but some prized amuletic treasures display a portrait of the wearer crowning the traditional heart shape.

Abracadabra: Abracadabra may seem to be merely a generic stage magician's term; however, it was originally used as a magic formula for warding off illness. Both the word itself and its relation to curing sickness are ancient, evolving from the Chaldee *abhadda kedabrah*, "Disappear, O sickness, from this world."

```
A B R A C A D A B R A
A B R A C A D A B R
A B R A C A D A B
A B R A C A D A
A B R A C A D
A B R A C A
A B R A C
A B R A
A B R
A B
A
```

To work the charm, the word "abracadabra" must be written on paper, dropping a letter each line (as shown in the illustration) and worn around the patient's neck for nine days. After nine days, it is thrown backwards over the shoulder into an east-running stream. This formula is known as a "shrinking charm" and there are several others, including a Hebrew cure which uses the word *abrakala*. The idea was that as the formula diminished, so would the sickness. The Hebrew formula appears to have been highly regarded, as it was written with stringent instructions for its precise execution. The abracadabra charm had staying power, for it was again popularized in the Middle Ages to ward off the plague.

Abraxas: Abraxas evidently originated with Basilides, a 2nd-century Gnostic philosopher of Alexandria. His followers, the Basilidians, made Abraxas the chief of the 365 genies that ruled the days of the year. Persians and Syrians claimed Abraxas to be the most ancient of the gods. Another variation has Abraxas as a god above 365 orders of spirits which occupied 365 heavens. The lowest of these was the domain of the spirits ruling Earth.

Since the 2nd century, Abraxas has been found on many types of magical charms used to ward off evil. His physical being is portrayed as cock-headed with a knotted tail and snakes for legs, carrying a whip.

Acorn: The fruit of the sacred oak symbolizes the highest form of fertility: an enduring and potent creativity of mind.

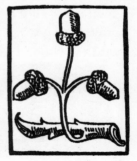

The acorn is widely considered to be a good luck charm; however, throughout time it has been employed for other purposes. For example, as an old European form of marriage divination a young woman would drop two acorns into a basin of water; if they floated together, a happy marriage was indicated. The

Druidic priests of the Celts consumed acorns as a prelude to predicting the future, and Scandinavians placed acorns in windows to appease Thor, god of thunder, as protection from lightning.

Aegishjalmur: A Nordic rune representing in Old Icelandic that which cannot be successfully opposed; irresistibility. The symbol was often painted on chests and shields or knitted into sweaters.

Agate: A wide variety of virtues have been attributed to agate. It is said to protect the wearer from all hazards, make warriors strong, speakers persuasive, cure insomnia and ensure pleasant dreams, avert storms, and offer protection and cure to almost any ailment. Agate is a stone of Mercury.

There are several types of agates, each with its own particular values. The red or "blood" agate gives protection against spiders and scorpions. The green agate cures any eye ailment, and it is said that if a woman drinks the water a green agate ring has been washed in, she'll never be sterile. Gray agate is worn around the neck to prevent stiff neck and ward off colic. The brown agate is the most powerful and

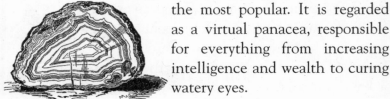

the most popular. It is regarded as a virtual panacea, responsible for everything from increasing intelligence and wealth to curing watery eyes.

In the middle of the 19th century, there was a tremendous demand for agate amulets in the Sudan. Black or brown agates with a white ring in the center were especially popular. The ring was regarded as an eye, and the amulets were worn to neutralize the Evil Eye or as a symbol of a guardian spirit watching over the wearer.

Alexandrite: The alexandrite is also a stone of Mercury, but to a lesser extent than the agate. It is a variety of chrysoberyl and was discovered in the Ural region of Russia. The alexandrite is distinguished by a beautiful pleochroism of green changing to red. Since red and green are the Russian national colors, the alexandrite is considered to be a stone of good omen in that country.

Alrune: The word alrune, which comes from the Anglo-Saxon meaning "secret," is used to refer to the mandrake root, or another hard root substituted for it, used in magic. It also refers to a small human figure fashioned from these roots and used as a good luck charm. In some cases, such a doll is carefully kept in a secret cupboard and consulted as an oracle. The dolls most likely originated in ancient Germany, where the word *alruna* meant a wise woman or seer.

Amber: Amulets made of amber have been used since antiquity. Ancient Greek poets metaphorically likened grains

A tree is identified as the source of amber in a medieval woodcut

of amber to the tears of grief shed by poplar trees or, in another version, by certain Indian birds. Another poet wrote that amber was the juice of the brilliant rays of the setting sun congealed in the sea. In any case, the beauty and malleability of amber, which is actually a fossilized tree resin, made it popular worldwide.

Perhaps in relation to its electromagnetic qualities, amber gained a reputation as a cure. It was said to protect the wearer from headache, toothache, rheumatism, any internal ailment, nosebleeds, and goiter. In many European countries amber is worn to ward off evil. Amulets carved into animal shapes have been found in Norway and in the Far East. It is believed that the animal forms enhance the power of the amulet and endow it with special qualities. Those found in Asia were thought to increase virility and fertility. Amber with natural markings or inclusions is highly prized.

Amethyst: The name of the clear purple or blue-violet variety of crystallized quartz comes from the Greek word *amethystos*, meaning "not to be intoxicated." However, the original significance of the stone is a bit more interesting than merely preventing drunkenness. It was the jewel

The Lorscher Ring, a dark purple amethyst set in gold is a treasured German antiquity dated to the late 10th century

worn by the High Priest during the initiation rites into the Eleusinian Mysteries in order that he might not become "confused, distracted or overwhelmed by the intense fascination of external phenomena." The secrets of Eleusis were never revealed, and eventually Dionysos, the god of wine, was worshipped there. During the Middle Ages the amethyst was not only called a wine stone but became associated with sacrifice. In this context the gem was an amulet of protection for both hunter and soldier. An amethyst placed under the pillow was believed to bring a sleeper prophetic dreams and to ensure their memory.

ANGELICA
*Angelica
archangelica*

Angelica: Angelica has been heralded for centuries in the folklore of Scandinavian countries as a protection against almost any disease imaginable, for purifying the blood, and as a remedy for poisons. The plant is also associated with pagan festivals of early summer. As an amulet, all parts of the plant are believed to be useful in neutralizing spells and enchantments.

Ankh: This symbol and amulet stands for "everlasting life." Scholars doubt that the Egyptians themselves knew how the ankh originated or why it gained its meaning, but every Egyptian god and goddess was depicted carrying the ankh. In its amuletic form of wood, metal, gemstone or faience,

the ankh gave its wearer the capacity to live life to its fullest degree and to enjoy successive lives for all time.

Apple: Immortality, love, and magic are associated with the apple. Nordic myths tell of gods who kept themselves eternally young by partaking of the golden apples of Iduna,  goddess of youth and spring. Welsh legend links apples and immortality, for kings and heroes were said to go after earthly death to Avalon, the paradise of apple trees. An ancient law from the *Triads of Ireland* demands the death penalty for felling an apple tree, signifying its sacred nature. As a symbol of desire and love, a golden apple was the prize won by the goddess Aphrodite, judged by Paris as the most desirable in the Greek myth. The connection between the apple and love persists to the present day in the phrase "the apple of my eye." Cut an apple in half crossways and you see a five-pointed star – sign of health and magic.

Arrow: As one of man's earliest weapons, the bow and arrow were regarded as a marvel. Such wonder has given them a place in magic and folklore. The arrow is also associated with the male, a symbol of power and virility. It is said that to give birth to a male a woman need only sleep with an arrow under her bed during her pregnancy. There are many celebrated bowmen of legend, Robin Hood the first among peers. From Robin Hood and the Golden Arrow:

Says Robin Hood, All my care is,
How that yon sheriff may
Know certainly that it was I
That bore his arrow away.

"Elf shot" is the term applied to a diseased animal believed to have been shot by an elf's arrow. According to a nineteenth-century Scottish superstition, "This deadly weapon the wicked fairy will throw at man or beast with such precision as seldom to miss his aim, and whenever it hits, the stroke is fatal."

Arrows are also associated with desire, and are no stranger to Cupid! And as Zeus, Thor and Jupiter have created their thunderbolts or arrows from the sky, the fairy folk have created earthly arrows with material goals in mind. From this we find that in Sweden as in Britain, arrowheads were carried as protection from elves. An association also exists between the arrow and the witch's athame, which implies direction of power and will. For those in need of protection from arrows, an ancient formula reads:

Ababa Omel alifal Cuttar uden et armoen
Trola Coblamot Fasteanus.

Ash: Ash has long been regarded as a sacred substance – not merely the remnants of a fire, but the seeds of the fire containing its very essence. Qualities associated with fire such as purification, strength, and life are also associated with ash. Burning is seen in many cultures as simply changing the physical state of matter, not as the destruction of the more spiritual qualities of that matter. This is not an archaic or isolated belief. Modern day Americans regard the ashes of cremated loved ones with reverence and often place the ashes in a special place in their home.

Ashes play a role in divination as well. In Lancashire, England for example, on the eve of St. Mark's Day (April 24) ashes were left on the hearth of a home overnight, and in the morning they were searched for anything resembling a footprint. The print was measured and the family member whose foot most closely matched was doomed to die within a year. A more lighthearted means of divination was employed in Ireland and the Isle of Man: on Halloween, bachelors would sprinkle ash along a quiet street and then stand back and wait. The first maiden to pass was destined to be the man's bride.

Aventurine: A type of quartz, usually green but occasionally can be found in yellow or even pink. Aventurine is not to be confused with "sunstone," a type of feldspar. When copper flecks are present, aventurine is often referred to as "goldstone." Known to promote creativity and imagination, intuition and leadership, this gem also offers opportunities in life, love and finances or careers. Through the ages, aventurine has also been treasured for its calming effect and is often used to fight anxiety. This effect is also of great benefit as an aid in meditation. Tibetans used aventurine in the eyes of sacred statues to symbolize divine sight.

Ba: The ba is an ancient Egyptian amulet termed the "heart soul," i.e., the soul of the physical body. It is a funereal amulet in the form of a human-headed bird made of gold and inlaid with stones. The amulet was placed on the breast of the mummy and was believed to protect the body from decay. Words from Chapter 89 of the *Book of the Dead* were recited over it, and under the influence of these spells the ba was thought to fly to the place of the gods as a representative of the deceased. Openings were left near the apex of the tomb to allow the ba free passage in and out. The

talisman was intended to allow the soul to link with the mummified body as well as with the spirit at will.

Basil: European folklore places sweet basil high on the list of love charms. Its scent alone is believed to excite a feeling of sympathy between two people. One old tale records how a young man on a journey of discovery is stopped in his tracks by a maiden from whose hand he accepts a sprig of basil. They fall in love and live happily ever after. Its magical quality may have come from India, its place of origin, where it has long been regarded as sacred, an herb to be grown in temple gardens. However, in medieval Europe basil came to be known as a plant of Mars with all that planet's negative character. Some old herbals remark upon a strong association with poison and scorpions. Despite the paradox, the Greeks still crown a bride with sweet basil in one of the world's oldest wedding traditions. The delightful aroma of its fresh leaves is enough to dispel dispiriting thoughts.

*BASIL
Osimum
basilicum*

Bee: The bee is the symbol of the sun, especially relating to fertility as it feeds and pollinates, reminding us to make our lives fruitful. The bee takes and the bee gives back. Since its flight is aerodynamically "impossible" in terms of its weight, the bee also serves as a symbol of accomplishment against odds, of patience and perseverance. Travel, friendship, devotion to family are all inherent in this insect's totem. The bee has been revered since ancient times, relating to Vishnu by the Hindus, the Eleusinian mysteries by the Greeks, wisdom by the  Celts and royalty by the Egyptians. Honey nourishes us and adds sweetness to our lives, and mead, honey wine, was the ambrosia of the gods. Royal jelly, prized as a cosmetic, is an essence produced by honeybees and fed only to select young bees who become the long-lived queens.

For the witch, bees are enormously valued for their wax, used in image-making and the candles recognized since Paleolithic times as especially powerful in sympathetic magic. Ritual beeswax candles should be placed in quiet places, away from TV or noise of any kind, and in a low-traffic area.

 Such candles should be cleansed before use to dislodge any "psychic debris" and should be "dressed" by oiling. By touching the candle as you oil, you are charging it with your own personal vibrations and concentrating the goal of your magic onto the wax.

Beryl: Beryl is a silicate of beryllium and aluminum. It is quite hard, and when it's transparent, quite beautiful. It occurs in hexagonal prism, commonly green or bluish green, but also yellow, pink, or white. The gemstone is associated

with the goddess of love, Venus, and the attribute most often mentioned is that it has the power to reawaken love, especially in couples who have been married for a long while. Beryl is also said to bring hope.

Bes: Bes is an Egyptian god who is invariably depicted as a squat, dwarfish, and rather ugly creature. He is the patron of fun and music, is said to help women in childbirth, and is considered a general good luck charm. Many amulets bearing his likeness have been found. Although Bes had no cult center in Egypt as the greater gods did, he was very popular and as a result holds a reputation as a "poor man's god."

Bes in the role of warrior

BETONY
Stachys officinalis

Betony: Betony is an amuletic herb said to be endowed with power against evil spirits. Because of this, betony was frequently planted in churchyards and worn around the neck. For centuries, the herb has been widely used for medicinal purposes as well – so much so that an old Italian proverb says, "Sell your coat and buy betony." Apuleius Platonicus in his *Herbarium*, which dates back to around 400 C.E., said this of betony:

"It is good whether for a man's soul or for his body; it shields him against visions and dreams, and the wort is very wholesome, and thus thou shalt gather it, in the month of August without the use of iron; and when thou hast gathered it, shake the mold till nought of it cleave thereon, and then dry it in the shade very thoroughly, and with its root altogether reduce it to dust; then use it and take of it when thou needst."

Betony does not grow wild here in America as it does throughout Europe. There are five species of betony, but the magical properties are attributed only to the *Stachys officinalis* or *Betonica officinalis* varieties.

Blood: Blood is associated with life force and no part of the body is as powerful as the blood. It is the primary indication of relationship. Sometimes we extend this bond of relationship to friends with a bloodshedding ritual, and we intuitively become blood brothers. Spilling of blood is a loss of power, and the signing of a document in blood is a commitment for life. Losing blood to an enemy puts you at great risk should the adversary know how to use your life force in a magical way. Protection

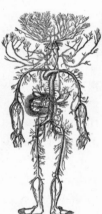

The arterial system

becomes necessary, and a counter charm should also use your own blood. A simple drop of your own life's fiery fluid adds power to any charm or talisman.

Bloodstone: The bloodstone is named for its appearance. It is a very dark green stone with tiny red flecks which resemble

A medieval jeweler suggests using bloodstone to prevent nosebleed

sprinkles of blood. The bloodstone is most commonly used as an amulet to guard the wearer against deception. It is also said to calm the angry. In the Leyden Papyrus, an Egyptian document of practical magic that dates to the 3rd century C.E., bloodstone receives the following praise for its amuletic properties:

"The world has no greater thing; if any one have this with him he will be given whatever he asks for; it also assuages the wrath of kings and despots, and whatever the wearer says will be believed. Whoever bears this stone, which is a gem, and pronounces the name engraved upon it, will find all doors open, while bonds and stone walls will be rent asunder."

Bone: Some societies do not view bone as simply a remnant of our physical being, but as the root of life since it is the longest-lasting part of the body. The indestructible nature of bone symbolizes resurrection. American folk medicine holds that bones have medicinal benefits to offer in the form of cures for a backache, toothache, or cramp. On some Pacific islands, bones are considered a bit more mystical and are used as magic wands. And certainly most of us have at some time broken the wishbone of a fowl for a wish.

Prehistoric necklace of human finger bones

Bread: In addition to being considered the "staff of life," bread is the subject of many interesting customs and superstitions. Bread  was used as a means of determining guilt in the primitive European system of trial by ordeal. Those accused ate a piece of bread and butter and if they choked were considered guilty. In many parts of the world, bread baked at home was used as a magic charm. In Belgium, stale bread was placed in the cradle to protect the baby. A century ago in rural areas of the United States, bread and coffee were placed under a house to keep ghosts out.

Perhaps because bread has always been such an important part of human life, it also plays a role in ceremonies concerning the joining of two people.

Bread was once used in the ritual of sealing a friendship in which the bread was eaten with salt. In France, brides would share a cake called the "bride's pasty" with their grooms  in order to arouse passion. The sharing of wedding cake between the bride and groom is still an integral part of our own culture's wedding ceremonies.

Many superstitions surround the way bread is eaten at a meal. In Britain and the United States, it is traditionally unlucky to take the last slice of bread on a plate; if the unfortunate soul who does so happens to be an unmarried woman, she is destined to remain a spinster. It is also believed that a loaf that falls upside down is bad luck. Sailors take this one step further, for in sea lore cutting a loaf and turning it upside down is enough to cause a vessel to sink.

Breath: Breath has been synonymous to soul or spirit for an extremely long time. The "breath of life" can be instilled or torn out of a being. There are stories of the gods breathing life into clay. But the belief is particularly intriguing in an Egyptian myth. When the torn and scattered body of Osiris is reassembled, Isis, the mistress of magic, breathes life into her husband. The story just "takes my breath away." To add power to an amulet or talisman, take a deep breath and hold it in while summoning the appropriate images that compliment the charm. Then slowly "breathe life" into the object in your hands.

Broom: This plant, not surprisingly, gets its name from the fact that its brushlike branches make it ideal for broom-making. It is prevalent on the sea coast and appears in early spring with bright yellow blooms. Very early on in European history, a sprig of broom in the cap of a soldier became a sign of success in battle. England's Henry II felt strongly enough about that association to give a form of the plant's medieval name, *Planta genista*, to his line of descendants, the Plantagenets.

BROOM
Cytisis scoparius

Caduceus: The caduceus is most commonly known as the magical staff of the Greek god Hermes, Mercury to the Romans. It's a winged staff with two entwined serpents, supposedly the result of the god's intervention in a fight between the two. It is an ancient symbol, possibly passed on to the Greeks by the Mesopotamians to

whom it represented the god who cured all illnesses. Hermes gave the staff to Asclepius, a mortal, who was deified as the god of medicine. The association between the symbolic caduceus and the art of healing persists to the present day, as it is the insignia of the medical profession.

Carnelian: Carnelian is a red stone held in highest regard by Mediterranean and Eastern peoples, who place great faith in it as an amulet against the Evil Eye and envy. Protection against envy is especially important, since they believe that envy can do great harm by stripping away that which is envied. When used for this purpose, the carnelian usually has a prayer engraved on it. The prophet Mohammed himself wore a carnelian ring. The carnelian seal shown below was found in the sand by Napoleon during his Egyptian

campaign. He always carried it with him, for the virtue of the carnelian also gives its owner the courage of his own convictions.

Carnelian is said to bring confidence and eloquence to those timid, or perhaps terrified, of public speaking. The stone is said to keep the wearer even-tempered and peaceful, and to increase sexual energy as well. For health, carnelian is worn as a remedy for unhealthy skin and for problems involving blood.

Cat's-eye: Cat's-eye is a gem mostly known as an amulet for wealth. It is used in money spells not only to protect the money one already has, but to bring in new money or even bring back money that has been lost. These characteristics make the cat's-eye an ideal talisman for gamblers. Cat's-eye is also used in rituals to maintain youth and beauty, and to protect the wearer from witch-

craft. Ancient Arabs believed that cat's-eye made its wearers invisible, and therefore gave them an advantage in battle. This stone, because of its appearance, is also said to benefit those with eye problems.

Centaury: Centaury is an herb said to have been discovered by the centaur Chiron, from whom the plant gets its name. The tiny pink flowers have five petals – the mark of a

CENTAURY
Erythraes centaurium

magic plant. Witches collect the blossoms, enclose them in tissue paper, and press them between the pages of a book. When three Moons have passed, the flowers are placed in a locket and worn for good luck. In addition, centaury is believed to produce "strange imaginings" when mixed with oil and rubbed on a candle. The familiar French *grimoire* of ceremonial magic, *Le Petit Albert*, says that when this is done "all that compass about it shall believe their heads to be in heaven and their feet on earth; and if the aforesaid thing be put in the fire when the stars shine it shall appear that the stars run one against the other and fight."

Chalcedony: This stone is a translucent quartz, usually milky white but sometimes a pale blue or fawn brown. Many Gnostic gems were engraved with the symbol of the Moon, for the stone's waxlike luster is moonlike. The Romans wore the stone as protection from the ravages of the Evil Eye, and it also combats negative magic. Chalcedony's element is water, and the stone is an amulet of safety from drowning as well as a safeguard for travelers, especially those crossing over water. The stone may be worn or carried as an aid in legal matters. Perhaps the primary benefit of chalcedony is its ability to bring tranquillity to a troubled mind. The stone is said to bring peace to a person and counteract the depressing, dispiriting influences of the planet Saturn.

Cimaruta: The cimaruta is a beautiful silver charm fashioned in the shape of a sprig of rue. Also incorporated into this charm are a crescent Moon, hand, key, heart, serpent, cock or eagle, fish, and a vervain flower. Not all of these appear on every cimaruta, but these are the most commonly found symbols. The charm's popularity flourished largely in 19th-century Italy. Most of the items that compose the cimaruta, including the silver it is made from, relate to the goddess Diana, who is deemed queen of Italian witches. Some consider wearing the cimaruta to be a sign of devotion to her, since it bears symbols of Diana. The cimaruta brings good luck, wards off evil, and protects against the Evil Eye. In the 19th century it was frequently placed around a baby's neck, to protect it since Diana is protector of infants.

Circle: The circle is an ancient symbol, separating the protected from the offensive. Within lies the realm of magic – a witch or magician performing a rite. Without lies the material world. This is both a world full of shades, ghosts, evil forces and all manner of disruptive spirits, as well as a kingdom subject to

Mohammedan Magic Circle

the powers conjured within the circle. Most often a circle is drawn beginning in the east, the place of sunrise, and movement is within a clockwise direction. The celestial power

*Magic Circle
of Dr. Faust*

originates here, and it is represented in our microcosm. The path of the sun becomes the outline of the magic circle. Walking the circle round is known as circumambulation. In cultures throughout the world, people dance in circular form. Witches perform the infamous circle dance to raise power while performing works of magic. In centuries gone by, ancient stone circles marked the sacred places. These hallowed sites represented a spiritual home for people of like belief and practice. The circle is also a ring of time as revealed by the clock, the zodiac and the wheel of the year. A circle drawn around yourself or a loved one is a mark of protection – thrice drawn, all the better. "Circle drawer" was a title given to sorcerers in 100 B.C.E.

Clover: Magic often favors a humble site. Common clover was once regarded as a holy herb with links to the dark goddess Hecate. The three-leaf form and obvious preference for the wild meadow rather than the confines of a garden echoed her themes of mystery. Old spell books named clover as trefoil and we find it listed along with vervain and dill, herbs of witchcraft. It is included among the herbs to fling upon Midsummer Fires. Trefoil was an herb to be collected, dried, and wrapped in linen as a love charm.

CLOVER
*Trifolium
pratense*

33

The good luck associated with the four-leaf clover is of relatively recent origin. Its rarity and symbolic cross pattern are possible reasons. Each leaf represents a gift for its finder: fame, fortune, a faithful lover, and health.

Coral: Coral is a protective amulet. It has been used in magic since ancient times. In their magic, the ancients would use only coral that had not been altered by human hands. Even today if a piece of coral being used in magic breaks, it is believed that its power is lost. Coral protects against sterility, violence, and the Evil Eye. It's also used to help rid one of violent thoughts and depression and to bestow courage and wisdom upon those who carry it. For centuries, coral has been associated with protecting children and guarding their health. One source says that coral can be used to bring luck to the home by holding it and, moving in a clockwise direction, touching it to every door, window, and wall, then placing the coral in a prominent spot.

The Brigit Cross is an Irish version of the corn dolly

Corn Dolly: Corn dollies are figures made from the last stalks of the corn harvest. Sometimes these figures are shaped like a woman and decorated with ribbons. The corn dolly is a charm to insure a good harvest the next year. It is usually kept until the sowing of next year's crop. The significance of using the last stalks of the harvest and of the doll itself come out of the ancient lore of the Roman goddess Ceres, the Earth Mother, who was believed to live in the fields and control all that grew out of the earth.

Cornucopia: "Cornucopia" literally means Horn of Plenty. Amalthea, known as the tender goddess, was a goat that raised Zeus on her breast milk. She was changed into a unicorn by Zeus after he accidentally broke off one of her horns. Regretting this accident, Zeus gave his mother back her horn. The tale of the cornucopia arose when all-powerful Zeus embodied the horn with the power to give its possessor the heart's desire. Frequent images of the horn filled with fruits and flowers abound. As a charm, an image or drawing of the cornucopia with the desire written on it should be carried at the time of the increasing moon.

Crystal: Crystals have been known to man since antiquity; however, their popularity has reached an all-time high in recent years. Ancient peoples believed crystal to be petrified ice. For thousands of years, tribal magicians and especially shamans have relied heavily on it as an essential tool. Crystals are primarily prized for their ability to increase psychic

power, and crystal gazing has long been employed as a means of divination by many cultures. Crystals should be purified before being used in magic to rid them of any negative charges they may have. Sea salt and infusions of sage and sweetgrass can be used to purify crystals, although there are many cultural variations. The light of Full Moon recharges the power of a crystal ball.

Dew: A simple gift from the elementals, dew will collect in the most unusual places. This can be gathered before the strong sun is too far above the horizon, warming the earth and evaporating the dew. Collect the precious fluid into a small jar and save for extreme emergencies of health. The cool dew can be placed on an ailing part of the body to bring soothing energy and the influence of earth and water to the difficulty.

Diamond: The diamond is the only gem composed of a single element. It is carbon in crystal form. Diamonds have been prized since the earliest of times and are the subject of a great deal of interesting folklore. Many ancient tales link diamonds with snakes or eagles. Magyar legend, for example, says diamonds are blown by thousands of snakes in caves, then buried by them to be found by some fortunate person. Legend also has it that diamonds have the power to reproduce themselves. In India it is believed that possessing large diamonds brings about misfortune.

Diamonds are thought to bestow courage and protection upon the wearer and were worn by Greek and Roman warriors for success in battle. Regarding relationships, diamonds are more than just the most common engagement stone. They are said to ensure fidelity, aid in the reconciliation of lovers, and relieve the causes of sexual dysfunction. The stone is especially effective when worn on the right side of the body.

DILL
Anethum
graveolens

Dill: Dill is an herb which is best worn in a locket. It has a reputation for being used in love potions, even though it was believed in medieval times to fend off the work of witches. Dill aids indigestion and is said to procure sleep, but its primary function is to ease nervousness and uneasy feelings. Its soothing effects have been used by generations of mothers to calm their distressed (and distressing) infants.

Distelfink: To outsiders, a curious practice of the Pennsylvania Dutch is to adorn their barns and doorways with colorful hex signs. A symbol commonly incorporated into these "magic circles" is the goldfinch, or as  they call it, the distelfink. The bird symbolizes good fortune and wards off evil.

Planetary symbol for Earth

Earth: The planetary Earth, representing the nurturing aspect of Mother Earth, is a benevolent symbol. It can be used to encourage support during troublesome times, especially in matters of the physical world. The Earth symbol reminds us to keep our feet planted firmly on the ground and take one step at a time. Development and growth are two characteristics that identify this planet's energy. Evolution is an ultimate end product. Draw this symbol on paper of earthy tones and place it where things need to develop and grow – in your garden, a child's room, your wallet or in baby's crib.

Egg: The egg is an ancient emblem of immortality, found in prehistoric tombs in Russia and Sweden as well as in many Egyptian hieroglyphs. The natural association between the egg and the beginning of life has led to the egg being regarded as a powerful fertility charm. In some countries, eggs are brought into the fields or carried with the seed

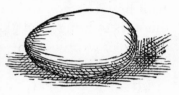

to increase crop yields. Eggs are believed to aid in human fertility as well, especially in Eastern cultures where they are used in ceremonies to overcome sterility and impotence.

In the Middle East, eggs are used to bring misfortune to one's enemies. The eggs are ceremoniously buried in the ground in a place where the intended victim is known to walk. One such charm is said to drive its victim insane.

Eggs have also been used by several cultures to protect children against the Evil Eye. For this purpose, the eggs are either passed over the child's head or broken on its face. Dreaming of eggs is said to be a good omen or to indicate a wedding. A dream of broken eggs indicates a lovers' quarrel.

ELDER
Sambucus nigra

Elder: Elder has long been associated with witches. Spirits and witches were said not only to live in the bush, but to be the bush. Scandinavian legend tells of an Elder Mother who watches for any injury to the bush. If any sprig is cut from it without first asking permission of the Elder Mother, whatever purpose the sprig is cut for will end in misfortune. The Elder Mother is said to give her consent by keeping silent.

Elder is worn or hung as an amulet. Russians believe it to banish evil spirits, and in Serbia it is used in wedding ceremonies to bring good luck. Crosses made of elder are hung on stables to protect the animals within from evil, and it is believed in some parts to offer protection from lightning. In Austria and northern England, an elder bush is made into the shape of a cross and planted at a new grave. If the bush flowers, it is taken as a sign that the deceased has found happiness in the otherworld.

Emerald: Emerald is a rich green variety of beryl. It is primarily associated with the goddess Venus, and meditating upon the stone is used in some religions to invoke her. Emeralds were revered by the Egyptians. One magical rite involved the consecration of a scarab carved out of emerald. It was put on a gold thread and worn as a charm. The Gnostic doctrine of Hermes Trismegistus, consulted by scores of medieval alchemists, was carved into what is known as the Emerald Tablet. The Moslems also used emeralds for amulets, carving verses of the Koran into them.

An emerald set en cabochon (uncut, but highly polished) was favored by European royalty during the Renaissance

Emeralds are said to protect expectant mothers and bring them safely through childbirth, strengthen memory, and help maintain chastity vows. Being attributed to Venus, the stone is a symbol of healthy romance and fulfilling love. It is said that emeralds lose their deep color upon exposure to lying, treachery, and evil intent.

Evil eye: Throughout much of Europe, the evil eye has an infamous history going back centuries. Belief in the evil eye continues to the present  in the Mediterranean, Central Europe, Africa, the Middle East, India, Mexico, Central and South America. Known as *mal occhio, mal'uocchiu, invidia* (Latin "envy"), fascination and other names, it is a belief system in which the human eye is able to send forth beams or rays that can cause harm. In today's urban populations, *mal occhio* is held responsible for physical illness, especially to children and pregnant women. The signal boded all kinds of bad luck. In rural areas, it is also blamed for blighting crops and harming stock, primarily dairy animals.

Traditionally the evil eye threatened what was most precious and most vulnerable – children, pregnant and nursing women represent the survival of the family, clan or tribe. When dairy animals' milk dried up or they lost their young, 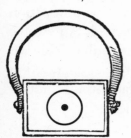 the family's means of livelihood was threatened. The loss of fruit trees and vines or other food crops to blight could ruin a small family living by subsistence farming.

Even today spells, charms, incantations, amulets, talismans and all manner

of superstition are called upon to prevent the evil eye from harming a loved one. The simplest of these would be to draw an eye on a piece of paper while maintaining the intention that you are safe and protected from all external harm. Put a scant amount of olive oil on the paper and carry the charm with you whenever you feel the need. Witches worth their weight in salt would never be caught without a charm against the evil eye on their persons.

Fatihat: Fatihat is a highly revered Muslim prayer. This first chapter of the Koran is called *fatihah*, which means "opening" in Arabic. It is probably the most frequently recited portion of the Koran. No solemn contract or transaction is ever completed unless the prayer is recited. An Arabic inscription and English translation of the fatihat is shown on the next page. It may be written on paper or engraved in metal or gemstone. Devotees carry the fatihat as a protective talisman, as well as to attract good luck.

In the name of Allah, the Merciful,
and the Compassionate.
Praise be unto Allah, the Lord of the Worlds.
The Merciful, the Compassionate.
King of the Day of Judgement.
Thee do we worship, of Thee we entreat for help.
Direct us in the path which is straight.
The path of those on whom Thou hast shown favor.
Not of those with whom Thou art angry,
nor of those who go astray.

Feather: To the ancient Egyptians, the feather represented Maat, goddess of truth and justice. In fact, the hieroglyph for Maat was an ostrich feather. The feather held great significance in the Judgement of the Dead. The dead person's heart was placed on one side of a scale and a feather was placed on the other; a perfect balance of the two

pans indicated that the person had been truthful. Osiris, who presided over the ceremony wearing a robe of feathers, would pass a favorable judgement on the deceased.

Feathers were very important to the Native American religions as well, as they believed birds to be mediators between god and man. Prayer sticks of tribes were decorated with feathers in the belief that the feathers would carry their prayers skyward.

Witches use feathers as a means of augury. Interpretations are based upon the colors and species of the feathers.

Fennel: Fennel is believed to have brought victory to the Greek warriors, and consequently it became a symbol of heroes and success. In the past, it was regarded as an aid to failing eyesight. Fennel is a very effective yet often neglected amuletic herb of protection. Dried seed heads may be woven into a wreath along with other protective herbs such as rue, rosemary, and dill and hung over the fireplace.

FENNEL
Foeniculum
vulgare

A dried bunch of fennel tied with scarlet yarn and fastened above the front door guards against intruders.

Fish: Everywhere that fish exist fish mythologies hook into the culture, sometimes for good, sometimes for evil. Mama Cocha, "Sea Mother," is the Inca goddess of the sea, source of all fish, worshiped by fishermen and sailors. On the Solomon Islands the *adaro* is a malignant fish/man. He travels along the rainbow and kills mortals by shooting poisonous flying fish at them. The *ikan tempel* of Indonesia is termed the "love fish" – dried and car-

ried as a charm, people believe it makes you irresistible to the opposite sex. The familiar fish symbol we see everywhere today was a pagan talisman long before its Christian association. The two twining arcs were identified with the Great Mother Goddess, the form depicting a sexual connotation.

The Christian church made wide use of the fish symbol. It was easy to draw and applied as a password graphic during times of Roman persecution. Followers of Christianity were called "Pisciculi," the root of the word deriving from "fish." The Bible makes use of fish allegory in numerous places. Disciples were "fishers of men," Jesus created "loaves and fishes," Jonah had an unfortunate experience with a marine beast. And according to John 21:6: "He said to them, 'cast the net on the right side of the boat, and you will find some.' So they cast, and now they were not able to draw it in because of the multitude of fish."

Fluorite: Fluorite is found worldwide and can be blue, yellow, green, white or purple. Occasionally it is called "flour-spar." Often admired for its fluorescence, it reacts brightly with ultraviolet rays or black lights. Sometimes called the "genius stone," fluorite aids concentration and higher thought, making it a perfect meditation device. It is also valued for use against various mental disorders. Fluorite aids with spiritual and cosmic insight, often relating to the third-eye chakra. The gem also combats sleeping disorders.

Often the colors have related attributes: blue for calming and inner peace, yellow for wisdom, green for order and abundance, white for purity and spiritual connection, purple for spiritual and mental awareness. Fluorite may be carried in your pocket or placed on a picture of someone who needs its favorable powers.

Frog: The frog is a symbol of abundance, fertility, and resurrection. A common Egyptian amulet, the frog was honored in tombs and occasionally even embalmed. The Egyptians associated it with Heqet, goddess of childbirth, and Central African women, believing it to possess strong fertility powers, eat the frog in order to have large families.

The frog is a widely used amulet, appearing in many different cultures both past and present. The charms are frequently crafted in metal, but are believed to be more powerful when made from coral and amber. Frogs themselves are widely used in magic, and they are believed to

possess aphrodisiac properties. For this purpose, a small bone from the left side of the frog's body is put into a drink or worn as an amulet. Pliny wrote of a preparation involving frogs which would render a man's wife completely disinterested in other men.

Frogs are the subject of a great deal of legend in Native American, Japanese, and Australian cultures. Most of these myths associate the frog with water or rain.

Fumitory: Fumitory is a member of the poppy family. It is one of the herbs believed to have greater power outside the garden, therefore witches collect it from fields and waste places. The name fumitory comes from the French *fumiterre*, meaning smoke of the earth. Legend has it that the plant does not come from seed but from the vapors of the center of the earth.

FUMITORY
Fumaria officinalis

It is the smoke of this herb that is noted for magical properties, although it is considered an amuletic herb to carry for protection. The primary magical use of its incense is purification. Dried leaves are crumbled over burning coals to purify an atmosphere. It is used in rites of consecration and to purify tools used in those rites. Fumitory is also used in exorcisms, as its smoke banishes and protects against evil spirits and spells.

Fylfot: Commonly known as the swastika, the fylfot is a very ancient mystic sign representing solar power, fire, life, and vigor. The symbol is found on tombs, monuments, pottery, coins, and jewelry dating back to the Bronze Age. The Scythians, a nomadic people of Eurasia, may have been the first to invest the fylfot with spiritual significance. Other cultures: Hindu, Chinese, Native American, Celtic, Greek, and Etruscan followed suit. The benevolent fylfot would appear on Buddhist statues in India and China around 200 B.C.E. As a Chinese hieroglyph, it stands for prosperity, good luck, and long life.

The fylfot was adopted as a symbol by right-wing German nationalists in the early 1900's. An adviser to Hitler suggested the counterclockwise version of the fylfot be chosen to represent their group, in light of the Buddhist theory that this particular version represented good fortune. Hitler, however, rejected this design and insisted upon its unlucky clockwise counterpart. Because of Hitler's decision in 1920 to employ the fylfot as his symbol, this ancient sign – which is believed to have traveled further than any other symbol in antiquity – is now overwhelmingly considered an icon for evil. Hundreds of centuries of meaning for this once-proud symbol have been completely eclipsed by its association with Hitler and Nazi Germany.

Garlic: Garlic, a member of the lily family, has an ancient reputation as a protective plant. It is primarily an amulet against negative energies and evil, though it is also believed to possess strong aphrodisiac properties. It is used in exorcism and purification rituals. Peeled cloves of garlic are said to rid a home of illness.

In China, Greece, Japan, and Turkey a garlic clove is carried as an amulet. The ancient Greeks put garlic at crossroads as an offering for Hecate, goddess of the underworld and witchcraft, who was said to be found there. It was considered sacred to the goddess Cybele, although her worshippers were not permitted to consume it. Egyptians believed it to be a religious plant and invoked it at the taking of oaths. Garlic is probably most famous for its use in warding off vampires. Eastern Europeans hung it in their homes as well as around their necks to keep them away. On Midsummer Eve the rural French would roast bulbs of garlic and give them to their families for protection. Medieval lore assigns garlic to Mars.

Garnet: The garnet is thought to provide the ability to hold true fidelity, friendship, and love and to keep one free from wounds. It is a protective stone believed to fortify the aura of its wearers, surrounding them with positive vibrations which will ward off any negative energy.

The ancient Egyptians found necklaces of garnet beads especially protective, and today the garnet is considered effective in warding off thieves. Garnet is also believed to impart strength to its wearer and should be worn during activities which are either physically or mentally demanding.

Garnets distributed through a mica schist

It is a stone of Mars, associated with the Temperance card of the Tarot.

GERMANDER
Teucrium chamaedrys

Germander: Germander is a member of the mint family. Its Latin name is *Teucrium chamaedrys. Chamaedrys* means dwarf oak, and the plant was so named because its leaves resemble those of an oak. This is of special interest in light of the magical significance of the oak tree as protector.

Germander has an ancient reputation as a cure for gout, though it is now primarily used to create ornamental borders in gardens. It is also valued today by many witches as a house plant.

Perhaps the most interesting part of germander's history is the fact that it was one of the primary herbs used in strewing. Strewing was practiced during the Middle Ages in Europe as well as by the ancient Greeks, who placed great stock in the ability of pleasing odors to preserve the health of both mind and body. Fragrant herbs were strewn on the floor of the main living area to mask the unpleasant odors. The health-giving oils of these herbs were stimulated as the leaves were pressed underfoot.

Gnostic gems: The Gnostics comprise religious sects which flourished between 250 B.C.E. and 400 C.E. in Alexandria, Egypt. The word *gnosis* means knowledge, and to the Gnostics it was an intuitive knowledge through revelation which would bring about salvation. Their beliefs were a blend of the religious and magical, with roots in Hebrew and Egyptian mysticism flavored by Greek philosophy. The Gnostics believed the world was full of evil and employed engraved gems as talismans to ward off harm.

These objects were cut in round, square, oval, and triangular shapes. They were fashioned from various types of semiprecious stones, of which black and green were apparently the most popular colors. It was believed that the stones possessed the powers of the planets and would bring the wearer health, wisdom, strength, and the ability

51

to absorb transcendental knowledge. Gnostic gems got their power not only from the stones alone, but from what was inscribed upon them as well. Gnostics believed that letters and numbers, commonly found on the talismans, possessed powers. Images of various gods also appear to aid the wearer in invoking the special properties and protections of a god through the talisman. Many of these talismans don't have much to do with the actual doctrines of the Gnostics and were worn simply to protect the wearer and to procure material prosperity.

Gris-gris: Gris-gris is a generic term for any object made sacred by ceremony. It originated as an African term for a protective charm. African slaves in the West Indies would call on a spirit whose help they wanted and ask it to enter an object, promising offerings and worship. If a spirit consented to take up residence in the object, a low hissing sound was heard. A gris-gris may be thought of as a container to hold a willing spirit.

A gris-gris is also used as a weapon. A small pouch is filled with certain herbs, roots, bones, or powders intended to cause harm. To find such an object at your door means someone has placed a curse upon you.

Hammer: A symbol of the worker, the hammer has been used throughout history to represent the working class, physical force, creation and power.

With Thor, for the first time a hammer is personified and given its own personal characteristics. The mighty thunder god's hammer even has a name – Mjolnir. Thor uses his weapon in the sky to create thunderbolts, much the same as Zeus effects in the Greek pantheon. Hammer charms are common, carried to bring strength and to ward off enemies.

Hand: The hand is the instrument which has propelled human destiny. It is the natural emblem of strength and power, having been man's first tool as well as his first weapon. The use of the hand in both blessing and cursing is indicative of the long-standing belief that psychic powers flow through the hand. It is perhaps the earliest symbol used in protective amulets.

A bronze magic hand dated back to the late Roman period (550 C.E.) is now in the collection of the British

Museum. This figure is known as the Blessing Hand since its first two fingers are up, as in the symbolic gesture of benediction. The Gnostic influence is clearly apparent in the occult symbols covering it: the winged caduceus, the frog, the serpent with a cockscomb on its head and the pine cone resting on the thumb. On the palm of the hand is a goat's head.

Among Arabs, the right hand, which is considered the "hand of honour," is represented in many figures and drawings as the Hand of Lady Fâtimah, a most powerful amulet. Fâtimah was the daughter of Mohammed by his first wife Khadijah, and she married Ali, Mohammed's cousin, and bore his sons, Hasan and Husayn. Mohammed considered her to be one of the most perfect of women.

The Hand of Fâtimah represents the whole religion of Islam and its fundamental duties. It also symbolizes the family of Mohammed, with the thumb representing the prophet himself, the first finger Fâtimah, the second her husband Ali, and the third and fourth their sons Hasan and Husayn. The fourth finger also represents many spiritual and moral qualities and virtues.

Hand of Glory: A gruesome example of the use of the hand in amulets is the infamous Hand of Glory, used between the 15th and 18th centuries, primarily in England and Ireland.

The Hand of Glory was intended for the protection of burglars during housebreaks, as it was said to prevent sleeping homeowners from awakening.

To make a Hand of Glory, the hand (right or left) of a hanged criminal was cut off and then wrapped as tightly as possible in a winding sheet and squeezed to draw out any remaining blood. It then was placed in an earthenware jar with a mysterious powder called *zimort*, saltpeter, common salt, and peppercorns – all pounded – and left in the jar for two weeks. Then the hand had to be extracted and exposed to the heat of the sun during the "dog days" of August or, if the solar warmth was insufficient, the hand could be dried in an oven heated with fern and vervain. This was done to extract all grease, which was then combined with virgin wax and sesame from Lapland to create a special candle to be used on the Hand of Glory.

When the candle was finished, it was wedged between two fingers of the hand. Sometimes in the absence of a candle one of the fingers of the hand would be lit instead. Whoever was shown this grisly object was said to be stupefied by it – deprived of motion and speech. Thus the burglar was free to rob the house without interruption. The flame could not be extinguished by any ordinary person, and the only substance said to extinguish it was milk.

It was said to be possible to destroy the influence of this grisly object by anointing the threshold of any entrance to the home with an ointment prepared during the heat of August and composed of the gall of a black cat, grease from a white fowl, and the blood of a screech owl.

Hawthorn: Hawthorn, also known as whitethorn or may, is the primary plant associated with May Day celebrations in France and Britain. It is believed to be a magical and protective plant. Hawthorn also has a long-standing association with betrothal. In Greece boughs were carried at weddings and some brides wore hawthorn wreaths; marriage-minded French girls used to adorn their windows with it; and in Britain, hawthorn was used in various forms of marriage divination. Hawthorn was regarded as a symbol of chastity by the ancient Irish.

HAWTHORN
Crataegus
oxyacantha

Legend associates this plant with fairies, although the nature of that association seems to vary from source to source. Hawthorn is said to protect against fairies and conversely to bring fairies into the house. It is believed to be exceptionally unlucky to bring the flowers of the hawthorn into the home or to gather hawthorn before the first week of May. It also offers protection against lightning. Hawthorn's thorns are used in some candle spells in which a device like a waxing moon or pentagram is drawn on the wax with the thorn itself.

HAZEL
Corylus avellana

Hazel: Hazel is believed to be a most powerful tree, magically speaking, and it has been used since ancient times in the making of magic wands and royal scepters. For centuries it has also been considered an extremely effective dowsing tool.

Hazel protects against evil and enchantment, and hazel rods are said to have the ability to actually force evil spirits to undo whatever they've set in motion. Hazelnuts are believed to ensure fertility. They are also used in a variety of forms of love divination. Celtic lore considers the hazelnut a "receptacle of knowledge," and eating the nuts is believed to increase mental powers and bring wisdom.

Hei-tiki: The hei-tiki is a curious, often bizarre carving of a human face or form that is worn around the neck as a protective amulet. It is Polynesian in origin, with most hei-tikis being employed by the Maori, who are members of the native Polynesian population of New Zealand. The amulets are usually made of jade and are supposed to represent a deceased ancestor. They are handed down from generation to generation.

Hei-tikis are highly valued not only for their ancestral significance, but also because of the circumstances surrounding the gathering of the jade from which they are made. A critical member of the jade-seeking expeditions was a wizard who would go into a trance after hiking to a region likely to have jade. While in this trance, a spirit would appear to him and tell him specifically where to dig. The hei-tiki would frequently be named after the spirit and carved in its likeness.

The charms were passed down to successive heads of the family. When the head of the family died, the hei-tiki would be buried with him and later exhumed by his successor. The finest examples of hei-tikis date from the late 18th century.

Hexagram: The hexagram is probably most recognizable as the Star of David, symbol of Judaism and Israel, although this identification did not become evident until after the 17th century. The hexagram actually has an ancient past as an occult symbol used to dispel evil. The two equilateral triangles that make up the hexagram represent the two major forces of the universe – the positive and the negative. The upward-pointing triangle represents the masculine element and fire, while the downward-pointing triangle represents the feminine element and water. The six-pointed star is also known as Solomon's Seal, the mystic symbol of the union of body and soul.

High John the Conqueror Root: High John was a mythic hero during the years of African slavery in the Americas.

Signifying a spirit of hope against all odds, High John brought joy, song, and laughter to the beleaguered people. The root that bears his name is most probably the sweet potato, a staple crop of the West Indies and our Southern states. It is the original potato, *Ipomoea batatus*,  producing an edible root rich in starch and sugar. Its twining high-climbing vine adorned with violet or pale pink trumpet flowers represented the virtue and quality of the godlike figure. The legendary root should not be confused with a similar Mexican medicinal root called "jalap."

As an amulet, High John the Conqueror root is carried in the pocket or purse to change bad luck to good, offset melancholy moods and confusion. It is said to bring success in any situation, encourage clear thinking, and renew hope and courage. Emancipation failed to dispel the need for supernatural help, and High John remains in the hearts of many African Americans.

 **Holed Stone:** Stones with naturally occurring holes in the center are said to be sacred to the goddess Diana, the protector of witches. They offer protection and work against black magic and nightmares. Holed stones are thought by some to possess healing properties and are rubbed along the body to absorb disease. Gazing through the hole of such a stone is said to produce visions of spirits.

Holly: Although associated with the celebration of Christmas, holly's use in midwinter festivities began with ancient magical crop rituals and later the celebration of Roman Saturnalia. It was used primarily for decoration and as a sign of rebirth. Holly is believed to be effective in warding off

evil, lightning, and enchantment and was also used in marriage divination, allowing unmarried girls to visualize their future mates. It is considered unlucky to burn holly while there's still any life left in it, to bring a flowering sprig of it into the house, or to step on its berries.

Honey: In Europe, Asia and Africa, honey was offered to the gods and as a libation to the earth and its spirits, often playing an important role in birth, marriage and death rituals. In ancient Babylonia, honey was regularly offered to the god Marduk and the goddess Ishtar to obtain their

help against the evils of witchcraft. Honey is a common symbol of abundance and fruitfulness in love and marriage. Some people believe that it is an aphrodisiac, as it has been used in love potions throughout Europe. A bit of honey given to a loved one enhances romance. It can also be added to love potions.

Horehound: Horehound is a protective herb native to Europe, though it has been naturalized in this country, particularly in California and Oregon. (It's rare to find it growing wild in the northeast.) There are two types of horehound, white and black; however, only the white has any magical significance. Horehound is associated with the Egyptian god Horus, and Egyptian priests called this plant the "Seed of Horus." For protection, the trailing foliage is hung as an amulet and the dried leaves are carried in a linen sachet.

HOREHOUND
Marrubium vulgare

Horseshoe: The horseshoe is considered a lucky and protective charm. For ages people hung horseshoes around their doors to protect their homes from witchcraft. Farmers fixed them to their stables to keep evil spirits from taking the animals out for night rides, which would leave them too tired for day work. It was believed that spirits had a strong aversion to iron and would not approach anything protected by it. The horseshoe should be fastened with the ends pointing up to prevent good luck from draining away.

Horns: Cernunnos, Faunus, Herne, Pan, Hathor, Isis, Cerne, Veles, and many other horned gods and goddesses adorned ancient pantheons. When the new religion of Christianity was born, the gods of the old became the devil of the new and the horns were "inherited" from these parent deities. Horns have been a symbol of plenty (*see Cornucopia, p. 35*). Evil spirits and demons have

been driven away by the sounding of a horn. In the military, segmenting the day or calling to duty is done by blowing the horn, or modern trumpet. Since before Christian times the shofar, usually a ram's horn, has been used during religious rites or to signal the end of a fast. Throughout history sexual vigor and male energy has been symbolized by wearing horns. For years fine scrapings of horn have been added to potions to stimulate this prowess. As an ironic symbol, in certain European countries "wearing horns" signifies a deceived husband. A small image of a horn may also be worn around the neck or placed under a welcome mat to keep away the evil eye or those who would wish you harm.

Hyssop: Hyssop is a highly aromatic plant that grows wild on our East Coast, although it was originally an alien plant which escaped from colonial gardens. Because of its strong aroma, hyssop was used in the past as a strewing herb. Magical uses include protection and purification. For purification it is used in bath sachets; as a protective amulet it is carried, worn, or hung in the home.

HYSSOP
*Hyssopus
officinalis*

Hyssop's flowers attract bees, and honey obtained from this source is said to be wonderful. The foliage of hyssop is so dense and hardy that it serves as a shelter for birds, rabbits, and other wildlings in winter.

Iron: Iron in its pure form falls from the sky as meteorites. This celestial origin resulted in its being considered a magical substance, a gift from the gods – the Egyptians credited Osiris; the Romans, Vulcan; the Teutons, Odin. Since ancient times iron has been used for protection and sometimes folk cures, a substance with healing properties used to draw out illness. Iron was the weapon of choice for repelling vampires or any evil spirits from a corpse intended to harm the living. Iron shavings were placed beneath a child's cradle, a person could feel safe wearing a necklace of

Alchemical symbol for iron

nails, and pieces of iron were placed around any threatened site. An exception prevailed among the early Gauls, who had drastic ideas about the metal. They considered it consecrated to the Evil Principal; one Egyptian historian had similar beliefs, calling it "the Devil's Bone." Hindus consider iron gifts unlucky. The most familiar usage down the ages, especially in rural places, was and still is the horseshoe, offering protection against evil spirits or harmful witchcraft. The horseshoe for amulet usage should be pierced with seven nail holes and affixed to the lintel of a door. Another protection method, "good for both adults and children," is to trace a circle around the body three times with a piece of iron. Carrying some iron is believed to increase physical strength, which makes it an excellent amulet for athletes.

Isis Buckle: The Isis Buckle is also known as the Tjet. It is an amulet made either of a red substance such as carnelian or red glass, or of gold, and is shaped in the form of the genitals of the goddess Isis. The amulet is worn by both the living and the dead and is said to impart to the wearer the virtue of the blood of Isis.

Isis is believed to be an intensely potent deity, possessing "words of power." She used her words of power to raise Osiris from death, and the Isis Buckle has a deep association with the dead. It is supposed to allow the deceased free access to anywhere in the underworld. The Isis Buckle is frequently inscribed with the 156th Chapter of the *Book of the Dead*, with which it is always associated. The words of that chapter follow.

The blood of Isis, and the strength of Isis, and the words of power of Isis shall be mighty to work as powers to protect this great and divine being, and to guard him from him that would do unto him anything that he holdeth in abomination.

Ivy: Ivy is a magically powerful plant associated with the Greek god Dionysos and the Roman festival of Saturnalia. Ivy has a reputation for diminishing drunkenness, although it was said to send the Bacchae into a frenzy and the priests of Jupiter into a prophetic trance. An ivy vine offers a home protection from evil and is sometimes used as a means of divination. The twining tendency of this plant is most likely the source of its ancient reputation as a symbol of fidelity. Dreaming of ivy is said to portend happiness. Ivy is also associated with poetry and inspiration.

IVY
Hedera helix

SHOU –
Chinese sign of
longevity

Jade: Jade takes its name from the Spanish *piedra de ijada*, which means "stone of the flank." In addition, one variety of jade is called nephrite, from the Greek *nephros*, meaning kidney. So not surprisingly, jade is believed to cure ailments of the groin and kidneys. Among Native Americans, jade is worn as an amulet against snakebite and is said to cure epilepsy. The stone also assists women in childbirth and strengthens the powers of the mind.

Jade is highly revered by the Chinese and is used in several talismans of good luck. The gift of a jade butterfly is frequently exchanged between a couple about to be married as a symbol of love, and a padlock-shaped talisman is placed around the neck of an infant to protect it from illness and bind the child to life. The stone is held in the hand during business deals to provide guidance.

Jasmine: This night-blooming plant has an understandable association with love, for its scent is hauntingly lovely befitting that tender emotion. Jupiter rules jasmine bestowing good fortune. Scores of love charms employ the dried blossoms of jasmine, which look like tiny white trumpets forming stars.

JASMINE
Jasminum officinale

Collect jasmine flowers on their third evening of bloom. Place them upon a thick layer of salt in a container with a tightly fitting lid. Add more salt until the flowers are completely hidden and cover quickly to let no air enter. Allow three days to pass while the container rests in a warm, dry, and dark atmosphere. Now gently remove nine blossoms and position

them in the center of a small white handkerchief of fine linen. Take up the four corners to form a pouch and secure it with a strand of bright red yarn. Carry the charm with you on love's adventure.

Jasper: This stone is nicknamed "rainbringer" for its ancient use in such ceremonies. It is believed to drive away evil spirits and not only to enhance mental functioning, but to steer the mind away from potentially harmful thought processes. Jasper, like jade, protects a woman during pregnancy and childbirth. It's also thought to relieve pain and protect against the bites of venomous creatures.

Phoenician seal cut in jasper

Jasper comes in a variety of colors, red and green being the most common. The Egyptians associated red jasper with the blood of Isis, and in the Middle Ages it was used for medicinal purposes in cases of extensive bleeding. Many charms for women are fashioned from red jasper. Green jasper is associated with general health and healing forces.

Jet: Jet is a black glasslike stone formed from fossilized wood. It is a protective substance which nullifies spells and charms and heightens psychic awareness. When powdered and burned, jet drives away snakes, alleviates pain, and is used in a form of divination. Many Italians wear amulets of jet to ward off the Evil Eye and nightmares. In ancient times, jet was highly regarded in the British Isles as a protection against any interference by evil spirits, and many wives would burn jet while their husbands were away on a journey in order to ensure their safety. The stone is believed to absorb part of the wearer's soul and therefore should be carefully guarded.

Juju: Juju is an African word for an amulet. It can be any object with protective magical symbols adorning it and is most often an object worn or used daily: a fan, the handle of a fly whisk, a necklace, walking cane, or toothpick holder. The word juju is sometimes used to refer not only to the amulet itself, but to the deities whose powers are invoked for protection.

Julbuck: Julbuck is a Swedish charm made of straw in the form of a goat. The charm stands about six inches high and is used for sympathetic magic to ensure good crops.

The goat has an additional magical significance in that part of the world. According to Scandinavian myth, the goat Heidrun provided intoxicating liquor for those heroes slain in battle and magically transported them to the warm and brightly lighted hall of Valhalla, where they enjoyed a pleasure-filled afterlife.

Juniper: Juniper is a small evergreen shrub, the blue berries of which are used to flavor gin. The plant is believed to offer protection and love. In medieval times, juniper was burned along with rosemary and thyme to purify the air inside a home or hospital and drive away infections during times of plague. It was also a critical ingredient in the preparation of *aqua vulgaria*, a healing water for wounds administered by medieval women to men returning injured from battle. Juniper offers protection from thieves.

.Frau Wachholder, the juniper spirit, is invoked to discover thieves by bending down certain branches. It is also used in some anti-theft charms. The shrub is venerated in Italy, Austria, and Germany as protection against evil spirits. Juniper planted at the doorstep

JUNIPER
*Juniperus
communis*

is believed to protect the home and prevent any evil spirit from entering. In Italy, branches of juniper are hung at the winter solstice just as holly is used in England and France.

Key: The key is an important magical symbol, representing access to a coveted place in either a physical or mystical sense. It is associated with the goddess Diana and is a critical element of the cimaruta, an Italian charm symbolizing devotion to her. The key relates to Diana in the form of Jana, an alternative form of her name, and her role as keeper of the gates of heaven and ruler of the doors and thresholds of a house. The key is also a symbol of Hecate, the mistress of the lower world who possesses the ability to open the gates and free imprisoned souls. Keys are also believed to be excellent conductors of psychic energies.

Knot: Knots are valued as potent tools in magic, whether tied for good or for ill. The witches' ladder, a widely used charm, is a string of nine knots, each tied with a feather in it. Knots symbolically fortify the aim or wish behind a charm; incantations are commonly recited as further reinforcement. Moslem soothsayers‧ prepare knotted

The Mystic Knot – Chinese Buddhist symbol

cords by blowing on the knots. In Victorian times, gold rings called lovers' knots were frequently given to women by their fiancés as a sentimental token of their love. Knots are tied at wedding ceremonies in many cultures to strengthen the marriage. To untie the knots of a charm is to undo its spell.

Kuthun: A kuthun is any item (a piece of jewelry, a book, anything) given by a witch at the time of death to another witch. The charm symbolizes the power which must be passed on. A witch cannot die until this is done. The kuthun is a legacy fulfilling a neophyte witch with spiritual and divinatory energy.

Ladder: Ladders are symbols of spiritual ascension and represent a passageway between the earth and the heavens. Belief in the ladder as a link between these worlds was strongest among the Egyptians. Many amulets in the form of ladders have been found in their tombs. The Egyptians believed that an immense iron plate formed the ceiling of the sky and the floor of heaven, and that there the gods and the blessed dead would live.

It was thought that the god Osiris ascended to this plate with the aid of a ladder. Horus the Elder and Set, the guardians of the ladder, would help the deceased to ascend. The ladder-shaped amulets were placed on or near the body of the deceased, and in later years priests painted a ladder on the papyri that were inscribed with texts from the *Book of the Dead* and buried in the tomb. Charms representing ladders have been found in some ancient Roman tombs as well.

Lapis lazuli: Lapis lazuli is a gold-flecked blue stone so beautiful that it is believed gods actually rejoice in inhabiting it and bestowing potent magical powers upon its wearer. It is

TSURU –
Japanese crane
of good luck

a healing, spiritual stone which increases psychic awareness, cures melancholy, and is said to strengthen eyesight. Lapis lazuli is used in some love charms and regarded as a highly effective fidelity charm. Necklaces of the stone protect the health of children and help to dismiss any frightening thoughts. In Macedonia, the stone was used as an amulet against miscarriage. Egyptians carved scarabs out of this stone, and Sumerian kings and queens fashioned cylinder seals from it. Lapis lazuli is a cherished gem in the Orient. The Chinese carve a traditional design of pomegranate and a bat on the blue stone to assure its wearer of a long, full, and successful life. Japanese of the Shinto faith choose lapis lazuli as the gem upon which to engrave the crane symbol above called *tsuru*, for good luck.

Laurel: The leaves of the bay laurel tree are used extensively in cooking today, but their significance goes far back to Greek and Roman mythology. As an amulet, the leaves are used to "bring forth" what is desired and to dispel negativity and evil. Bay leaves were chewed by the priestess at the Delphic oracle to enhance her prophetic inspiration. When placed under the pillow, they are said to induce prophetic dreams. As a means of purification, the leaves are burned and scattered over the area in question. Dried bay leaves play a major role in many love charms. In one such charm, they are scattered over live coals and as they burn, you are to envision the face of your beloved in your mind's eye, while chanting:

Laurel leaves,
Burn in fire,
Draw to me…
My heart's desire.

Lavender: The primary quality of this herbal plant is its fragrance, and it has been highly prized as a perfume since ancient times. Lavender is one of the nine herbs cast into the sacred fires of St. John's Eve to celebrate summer solstice in France, Spain, Portugal, and the British Isles. The age-old custom honors the Sun at its zenith on the longest day of the year. Lavender belongs to Mercury and the element of air. Spikes of its pale purple flowers are carried as charms to attract the opposite sex.

LAVENDER
Lavendula
officinalis

Alchemical
symbol for lead

Lead: Lead belongs to Saturn in the astrological correspondences of classical times. Saturn was then the faintest and slowest moving of the seven known planets marking the limits of the universe. Lead and the color black were representative of Saturn's supposed dark and malefic qualities, and leaden charms in those days were most apt to be concerned with evil intentions. Occultists of later centuries used lead for operations requiring patience and long-term results. The Magic Square of Saturn – nine

4	9	2
3	5	7
8	1	6

figures adding up vertically, horizontally, and diagonally to total fifteen – was engraved on a sheet of lead and carried as an amulet. Today lead is often employed as a protective token and used to guard valuables.

Lodestone: This mineral of natural magnetism, also known as magnetite, has long been regarded as a magical tool with a living force dwelling within it. It has an age-old affinity with water, and keepers of the lodestone regularly place it in water to renew its vitality. The metal's power to attract iron and other substances led to its use as a charm to draw good fortune. In the West Indian belief systems of Voodoo and Obeah, two lodestones are carried in a red pouch – one to drive away evil and the other to bring good luck.

Lotus: In ancient Egypt the white water lily blooming on the Nile was symbolic of that river's gifts of fertility, and came to represent the female principle of life. Deemed too sacred a symbol for individual amulets or personal decoration, the lotus was reserved for temple and tomb architecture and wall paintings. It later appears on Gnostic amulets in association with Isis, in

Egyptian lotus – sign of Earth

The egg and lotus signify health and eternity in the Brahman faith of India

her role as nurturing mother, and Horus the Child, who symbolized the rising Sun. (Horus was known to the Greeks as Harpocrates, their god of silence.) Hindu myths hold the lotus sacred to Lakshmi, who, as the wife of Vishnu, is the goddess of prosperity, beauty and grace. The Chinese revere the lotus as the emblem of purity.

Malachite: A blue-green stone, the pattern of which resembles wood grain. It makes a good amulet for children, as it is believed to protect them from harm and to ease teething pain. The image of the Sun is frequently engraved upon this stone to fortify it with extra power. As the Sun is regarded as a deadly enemy to demons, the engraved malachite is a powerful talisman against enchantment and evil spirits. Malachite protects its wearer from falling and is said to warn of approaching disaster by breaking into pieces. This stone also draws love to its wearer and is commonly used in love spells; additionally, it keeps depression at bay and promotes relaxation. Malachite is considered an ideal success talisman for business and salespeople and is a guardian stone to travelers.

Mandrake: Mandrake is the oldest known narcotic plant. It is valued primarily for its roots; however, since actual mandrake plants are rarely seen today outside botanical gardens, its magical use has diminished. The ancients used mandrake as an aphrodisiac and to combat insomnia and depression. It was also believed to have powers against

MANDRAKE
Mandragora
autumnalis

demonic possession and to grow only under the gallows of murderers. Great care, along with elaborate ritual, was used in extracting the root as it was said to resemble the human form and to utter a bone-chilling shriek when uprooted. In the 16th century, puppets fashioned from artificial mandrake roots (bryony roots) were thought to possess magical powers and sold for a high price. Mandrake reputedly remedies sterility in both men and women. Its amulets were placed on mantelpieces in Victorian England to avert misfortune and ensure a happy and prosperous home. Bits of the root were often used in protective sachets.

MANDRAKE ROOTS
Hortus Sanitatis,
Johannes de Cuba, 1498

Mezuzah: This is an ancient Judaic talisman still found in the homes of many Jews. Parchment inscribed with verses from Deuteronomy is encased in metal or wood and hung by the front door to remind the faithful of God's law. Those entering or exiting the house touch the mezuzah, then press their fingers to their lips. Mezuzah means "doorpost" in Hebrew.

Mirror: The mirror has come a long way from the centuries-old method of gazing into still water. Through the years reflection devices have evolved from still ponds to polished metal and on to the glass mirrors of thirteenth-century Venice. No matter how you look at it, a mirror has always symbolized the search within. This is a looking back to one's inner self or one's past to help make sense of a disturbing situation that exists in the present time. A gaze into the future by way of the seer or scryer is also a legendary use of the mirror. The reflection can change its shape and show the viewer images of friends, loved ones, even of far-off places. The reflection is also the soul, and with this understanding comes the belief that our soul is separate from the body and knows no boundaries. The soul can see and experience the past, present and future. A broken mirror is said to be a sign of seven years' bad luck. At the very least such an accident is a sign of trouble to come, but possibly of death inevitable. A chip of glass from a broken mirror is frequently used in spells of retribution or discord. The mirror is also used to ward off the evil eye. If you have trouble with a neighbor, turn a household mirror to the direction of the disturbing force and wait to see the negativity turn back upon its source.

Mistletoe: Mistletoe is a parasitic plant which grows from the bark of trees after its seeds have been deposited there by birds. The plant was revered by the Druids and considered most magical when attached to the oak tree. On the sixth day of the waxing moon, Druids clad in white robes would ceremoniously search for mistletoe, then cut it from the tree with a golden knife. The falling branch was caught in a white cloth. If the mistletoe touched the ground it indicated great misfortune to come. Then two white bulls were sacrificed to endow the highest magical properties to the branch. The mistletoe was infused in water, then consumed by the Druids as a cure-all or used as a charm against all evil. They also used it in their fertility rites.

Mistletoe is Sir James Frazer's "Golden Bough." In Norse legend, the much beloved god Balder was slain by an arrow made from the

MISTLETOE
Viscum album

hard wood of mistletoe. The god was later cremated, and Frazer believes this myth was enacted at Midsummer festivals in Scandinavia by primitive rites involving human sacrifice. Mistletoe is still a part of Midsummer festivals where, as an evergreen, it represents life. In classical mythology a branch of mistletoe, sacred to Persephone, served the Trojan hero Aeneas as a passport to the underworld.

This plant is considered a fertility and good luck symbol which is commonly hung in homes during the winter holiday season. A kiss under the mistletoe is a centuries-old custom. Mistletoe is called by some the "shrub of ghosts," for it is said to enable one not only to see ghosts but to make them speak. A withered, yellow mistletoe branch was thought to possess the power to uncover buried treasure.

Moonstone: The moonstone is a gem named for its silvery white, moonlike appearance, which seems to change with the movement of light. Eastern belief holds that a living spirit actually dwells within the stone and that it is a gem of good luck. In India it is considered sacred and is never displayed for sale unless it is set upon a yellow cloth; yellow is considered an especially sacred color. Moonstone is a great stone for lovers, since it is believed to arouse feelings of love. Also, if the stone is placed in the mouth at Full Moon, lovers are thought to be endowed with the power to read the future of the relationship – for better or worse.

MUGWORT
Artemisia vulgaris

Mugwort: This plant is the hero of the weary traveler, as it is said to prevent fatigue. It is also known as St. John's Herb, because during his sojourn in the wilderness St. John was said to have worn a girdle of it to fight fatigue and to protect him from wild beasts. If gathered on St. John's Eve, the plant reputedly offers protection from disease and misfortune. Crowns of mugwort were worn on this day, and when purified in bonfires and placed over doors they are believed to ward off evil possession.

Mummy Beads: The Egyptian passion for jewelry included unique designs made of faience beads strung on linen threads, so valued that they found their way into the sarcophagi of mummies along with gemstones. Some have reached us, two thousand or so years later, termed "mummy beads" and venerated as amulets. Faience, a quartz-based ceramic in brilliant colors, was often embroidered into rows for collars, bracelets, belts. In 2005 archaeologists made the most amazing of all beadwork finds, dating from about 4,200 years ago — a net of beads fully covering the mummy that perfectly reproduced the face and body of the deceased. The jewels of choice were often lapis-lazuli and carnelian, the

Ancient Egyptian necklace found on a mummy

gorgeous blue and orange sometimes teamed with smoky topaz and other colors. Gold was a favorite as well, often hammered into beautiful natural designs of dolphins, leaves, flowers. All accompanied the mummies, their encased figures awaiting to join the sun in its daily cycle. Mummy beads of such ancient yesterdays may offer particular magic. Some

such amulets are available in galleries dealing in antiquities; other shops offer reproductions of Egyptian mummy beads.

MYRTLE
Myrtus communis

Myrtle: Oddly enough, myrtle is considered an emblem of love and new beginnings on the one hand and the "tree of death" on the other. In Greek myth it is tied to the death of kings; however, as an evergreen it has also been associated with the theme of resurrection. In the Mediterranean, myrtle is sacred to the love goddess Aphrodite, and generally the plant is connected with love, fertility, and marriage. Legend has it that no woman who is destined to remain a spinster can make myrtle grow. When founding a new colony, Greek emigrants would bring boughs of myrtle with them to symbolize the ending of an old cycle and the beginning of a new one.

Nails: The talismanic use of nails is an ancient and widespread custom. Romans believed the driving in of a nail was an act of protection against sorcery and fascination, and Greeks placed nails in tombs as amulets for the dead. Many of the ancient nails were inscribed with magical symbols, each of which offered protection from the Evil Eye in its own right, thus making the nail a most potent charm.

An age-old method of killing or injuring an enemy was to inscribe his name on a piece of lead, wax, or pottery and drive an iron nail into the name, add an appropriate curse, and bury it. Another method was to drive a nail into the footprint made by your enemy and hammer it in with a stone while saying, "Cause harm to _____ until I remove thee."

Naoratna: The naoratna, or "nine-gem" jewel, is probably the most valuable and expensive charm ever devised. It is Hindu in origin and is designed to combine the powerful astrological influences of the Sun, Moon, Venus, Mars, Saturn, Jupiter, Mercury, Râhu (The Dragon's Head or

*Chandra, Hindu Moon god,
expelled from heaven to circle
the night sky forever*

ascending node) and Ketu (The Dragon's Tail or descending node). Nodes, from the Latin *nodus*, refer to the points of intersection of the Moon's and Earth's orbits. Hindu astrology considers lunar influences to be of vital importance. The nine gems were originally intended to comprise one ring; however, sometimes they were set separately in a series of rings to be worn corresponding with the days originally named for celestial bodies. An old Hindu treatise on gems describes the manner of composing the setting of the naoratna in the following way:

In the center	*Surya*, The Sun	Ruby
To the East	*Shukra*, Venus	Diamond
To the Southeast	*Chandra*, The Moon	Pearl
To the South	*Mangal*, Mars	Coral
To the Southwest	*Râhu*, The Dragon's Head	Jacinth
To the West	*Shani*, Saturn	Sapphire
To the Northwest	*Brihaspati*, Jupiter	Topaz
To the North	*Ketu*, The Dragon's Tail	Cat's-eye
To the Northwest	*Budh*, Mercury	Emerald

Such is the planetary setting.

Many of the gems chosen to correspond with the celestial bodies differ from Western assignations, and some more modern examples of the nine-gem jewel trade the jacinth, pearl, and cat's-eye for zircon, amethyst, and carbuncle.

Since the Hindus believed that the virtue of every gem depended upon its perfections, only the very rich could afford this talisman.

 Nefer: This is an ancient Egyptian amulet made in the form of a stringed musical instrument. It was always red, made of carnelian or some semiprecious red stone or red porcelain. The nefer is believed to bring its wearer good luck and happiness. The amulet, which enjoyed extreme popularity, was usually strung with beads on a necklace or worn alone as a pendant.

Oak: The oak is symbolic of strength and long life. Of all trees, the oak reigns supreme in Occidental cultures. It is associated with no less a deity than Zeus himself; his oracle at Dodona was in the form of a sacred oak whose rustling leaves transmitted the god's answers to questions. Oak wood kindled the festival fires

of Celts, Germans, and Slavs. Groves of oak were the temples of the Druids. Small wonder that the wood, bark, leaves, and acorns of the oak came to be charms of magical power. A perfect oak leaf collected at summer solstice, dried, and placed in a wishing box made of oak speeds fulfillment of desires. In bygone days witches wore necklaces of acorns in divination rites to protect themselves from being overwhelmed by the forces of darkness. A small square of oak bark placed in wallet or purse is said to discourage theft.

Obsidian: A volcanic glass formed when lava meets the water. Most obsidian is black, but red, brown and even green and blue have been found. The stone is also called "Apache tears" in North America and "Pele's tears" in Hawaii. The name originates from Greece, meaning "vision," possibly because obsidian was often used to make mirrors.  Chipped obsidian is extremely sharp and was used for arrowheads and cutting implements. It is known as a stone that, like it or not, would show the truth about oneself. Carrying obsidian helps to ground and balance. Snowflake obsidian is particularly good for balancing spirit, mind and body, and it excels for breaking bad habits to form good ones. Obsidian is also employed to protect, guide and bring visions. The stone is a first rate tool for divination and scrying.

Athena, Greek goddess of war and peace

Olive: The olive tree has long been regarded in many parts of the world as a symbol of peace. Extending an olive branch to someone signifies an attempt to make peace. The olive tree, sacred to the Greek goddess Athena, has a long history of beneficial magic. Oil from the olive tree is an essential ingredient in many charms and rites promoting reconciliation.

Onyx: A quartz gem with bands of black and white, brown and white, or completely black, the onyx has a sinister reputation. Medieval texts regard it as a gem of Saturn and say it will create strife, cause melancholy, and produce bewildering dreams. In India, it is worn around the neck to subdue love's passion. The Arabs called the stone *el jaza*, "sadness." Witch lore records a kinder attitude, especially toward the all black variety of onyx. The gem is worn in the performance of rituals at Dark-of-the-Moon and to ease the pain of childbirth.

Medusa from the onyx patera, Naples Museum

Opal: The reputation of the opal as an unlucky stone is of comparatively recent origin. George F. Kunz, an authority on gems, suggests it was due to an enchanted heroine in one of Sir Walter Scott's novels whose misfortune was equated with the opal she wore. Kunz adds that the opal's brittleness and frag-

87

ile nature made lapidaries and gem-setters of two centuries ago reluctant to work with the stone, and the superstition grew out of their prejudice against it.

The opal was held in high esteem by the ancients and regarded as a powerful amulet of protection against disease.

A courtier holds the Holy Roman Emperor's crown

Another of its magical qualities is recounted in Plato's *Republic*, where a magnificent opal set in a ring is turned inward to the palm and renders its wearer invisible. Pliny, in the 1st century of our era, departs from the usual dry style of his volumes on *Natural History* to extol the beauty of opals: "for in them you shall see the living fire of the ruby, the glorious purple of the amethyst, the green sea of the emerald, all glittering together in an incredible mixture of light." Albertus Magnus, the medieval philosopher, writes about the opal set in the crown of the Holy Roman Emperor which "guards the regal honor."

The virtues of the opal are only now beginning to regain prominence. It is said to stimulate psychic power by opening the inner eye and is used successfully in meditation and divination. The black opals of Australia have since their discovery in 1900 been considered as exceptionally lucky gems.

Orpine: This is one of the herbs brought by early settlers to this country for its magical properties alone, as it is without culinary or medicinal value. Listed as an alien plant in wildflower guides, the orpine (*Sedum telephium*) blooms year after year along roadsides and in old meadows. You may look in vain for a mention of orpine in herbals of the past or present. However, references turn up elsewhere. The English historian John Stow in his *Survey* (1598) describes flo-

ORPINE
Sedum telephium

ral decorations hung up in London on St. John's Eve (summer solstice) saying, "And every man's door was shaded with green birch, long fennel, St. John's wort, orpine, white lilies, and the like." A folk name for orpine is "midsummer men." A Book of Shadows privately kept in the early years of this century advises a maiden with romance on her mind to "collect a single blossom of orpine in silence on the Eve of St. John and sleep with it beneath your pillow in order to dream of the man who will one day love you."

Ouroboros: The ouroboros, a circle formed by a snake or serpent biting its own tail, is a major occult symbol dating back to the Gnostics in Alexandria around the turn of the Christian Era. Alchemists frequently used the symbol, and in the earliest

From Chrysopeia, an alchemical text, 4th century

treatises the emblem is accompanied by the Greek phrase *en to pan*, "all is one." The ouroboros symbolizes totality as well as the continuing cycle of nature and renewal. A snake swallowing its own tail forms a circle, a complete whole that is also a hole, zero, nothing. Nothing is everything. The end is the beginning. Some versions of this symbol are half black and half white, underscoring the theme of balance between opposing principles.

Owl: The bird has as mixed a bag of mythologies as could be imagined. At its most positive it is wisdom's heir, "as wise as an owl," the symbol of Mensa. An owl is an attribute of Athena, the goddess of wisdom. The Hindus consider a white owl the vehicle of Lakshmi, goddess of wealth, and good luck near a home. In ancient Peru the owl was worshiped and often depicted in art. But most cultures consider it a bird of ill omen, often of poverty and death. In ancient Egypt the owl was the hieroglyph of the sound "m," often drawn with broken legs to keep this bird of prey from coming alive. The Hopis considered the owl taboo, an attribute of evil sorcery. Aztec artists depicted Mictlantecuhtli, the god of death, accompanied by owls. The Mayans had a similar belief, describing owls as messengers from Xibalba, the "place of fright."

Greek Owl of Wisdom

Some cultures have conflicting feelings about owls – in Japan depending on species. Some owls were perceived as divine messengers of the gods; others, including barn and horned owls, were considered demonic. The French consider the *hiboux*, eared owls, symbols of wisdom, but *chouettes*, earless owls, bode no good. To the Malays owls are all simply *burung hantu*, ghost birds. The Finns are more paradoxical. They view the owl both as a wisdom symbol  and symbol of stupidity because of its "dumb stare." As for our own usage, we prefer to enjoy owl charms as emblems of wisdom and prosperity.

Patience Stones: These are pebbles from a stream or the sea worn smooth by friction with other stones and moving water. Possibly of Saxon origin, they were well known in England from the early Middle Ages. This amulet is meant to comfort those in distress and relieve anxiety when held in the hand. Patience stones should be found and presented as a gift to another by the finder. Ideally, the stones should be dedicated to the recipient during a waxing moon and presented the night before a Full Moon.

Peacock Feathers: Held in high esteem as good luck in India, but in Europe considered a symbol of ill will. This could be due to the fact that the peacock is associated with the Greek goddess Hera, wife of Zeus, who was portrayed as jealous, vengeful, and cruel, or perhaps because its "eyes" represent the Evil Eye. Hindus and Moslems, however, believe peacock feathers ward off evil. Burying the feathers with an object was once thought to prevent its decay.

Pearl crescent and swallow brooch

Pearl: Beneficial, protective, and akin to the Moon, the pearl represents the soul and the mystic center of the personality. It was the favorite jewel of the goddess Venus, and accordingly the ancient Romans wore pearls in their hair to ensure romantic success and dissolved the stones for use in love potions. Moslems and Christians have associated the pearl with heaven. Chinese tradition holds that it symbolizes "genius in obscurity."

Pentagram: The pentagram is a five-pointed star especially associated with ceremonial magic. It was thought to offer strong protection from evil and was used to guard windows

92

and doors as an amulet for happy homecomings. This ancient symbol was used by the Mesopotamians, the Gnostics, the Celts, the Pythagoreans, who considered it an emblem of perfection. Early Christians believed it represented the five wounds of Christ. It has been taken up by current witches and is frequently used as a New Age symbol. Though it was not always the case, the inverted pentagram is now widely considered to represent evil. The pentacle can be in forms other than the star; the term also refers to circular talismans used in ceremonial magic.

PERIWINKLE
Vinca minor

Periwinkle: Delicate pinwheels of lavender-blue flowers, their five petals forming a star in its center, set amid a bed of shiny evergreen leaves, are an enchanting sight. It's clear to see why medieval French herbalists called periwinkle *violette de sorcier*, the sorcerer's violet. Today commonly known by its Latin name of *Vinca minor*, the creeping plant has become a popular ground-cover. But long ago it was a sacred herb of Venus and renowned for its power to revive fading love, expel evil, and channel wayward thought. Strict rules applied regarding how and when to gather periwinkle. One old source declares that the Moon must be waxing in the sign of Taurus. Another advises, "And when thou shalt pluck the wort thou shalt be clean of every uncleanliness, and thou shalt pick it when the moon is nine days old." An alien plant in America, the periwinkle (also known as ground-myrtle) escaped its colonial gardens and thrived in wild environs.

Phallus: Primarily considered a fertility amulet, the use of this symbol goes back to prehistoric times and is still prevalent today. The phallus symbolizes life force, creativity, and active power. Many cultures worldwide considered the phallus a sacred amulet, but it was especially prevalent in ancient Egypt, India, and Rome. Phallic amulets protect the wearer from malice, envy, and evil influences in general.

Pomander Ball: This is a protective amulet in the form of a perforated ball of filigree bone or metal which contains fragrant dried herbs and resins and is small enough to wear as a pendant. Although often they were worn simply to provide relief from foul odors, pomanders also aided the health of the wearer, particularly in crowds. They were filled with antiseptic herbs such as lavender, rosemary, and thyme which helped defend against contagious illnesses. Another version of the pomander is any citrus fruit studded with cloves and hung by a door to protect the home.

Poppet: "As above, so below" is the basic principle of sympathetic magic, achieved when one object is likened to another. In this case a doll is made in the image of a living being – the two become one. What is done to the poppet is also done to the living person. Ideally a poppet would be fashioned of the worn clothes of its subject. This outer garment would be stuffed and personal objects would be sewn into the body. Hair, semen or fingernail clippings would work, but the preferred link would always be blood – the source of life and without which the individual could not live. Once fashioned, the poppet would be named during the enchantment of the image, after which the poppet becomes the intended. Poppet magic is frequently combined with other magic. For example, a healing ritual can be performed on a poppet in the image of a sick person. Poppets can also be saved over time and remain functional. It is best when not in use to keep them in a small wooden box that also contains personal objects of the individual, such as letters, clothing or other small private items.

Quartz: A very hard mineral found in rocks all over the world; the second most common mineral found in the Earth's crust. The ancient cultures considered it to be of magical value in its many varieties: agate, chalcedony, opal, and especially rock crystal. Those who use crystals metaphysically believe that they amplify positive energies, and employ them in meditation as well as for grounding and protection. The various shapes and colors of quartz crystals are believed to have their own distinct properties. *See Crystal, p. 35.*

Queen Elizabeth Root: A device used as a divinatory tool in Voodoo and Obeah lore. Any root of appropriate size that can perform as a pendulum may serve the purpose. After the root is chosen and the dirt shaken from it, a thread measuring two hands long is tied around one end. Holding the other end of the thread between thumb and forefinger, the practitioner suspends the root and waits until it is motionless. A question is asked, aloud or silently. If the root moves from left to right or in a circle, the answer is affirmative. Its royal name was given as a term of respect for the supernatural forces dwelling within a root, vital to the nourishment of a plant.

Rainbows: "Yokwe" is a lovely greeting from the Marshall Islands, akin to the Hawaiian "aloha." The two syllables mean "you" and "rainbow," and the word indicates that "You are

beautiful like the rainbow." According to Genesis, after the Flood God gave the rainbow to the world as a promise that He would never again destroy it. When Moses ascended Mount Sinai to receive the tablets, observes the Zohar, the rainbow took off its garment and presented it to Moses as a protection with God.

Myths from many cultures equate rainbows with serpents; both symbolize immortality and water, especially rain. Khonvoum, supreme hunter god of African pygmies, carries a bow of two snakes that appear to mortals as a rainbow. When the sun sets, the god gathers pieces of the stars and throws them at the sun so that it may rise the next day. Basques believe that Ortzadar is a spirit guide for the dead. When a person dies and the soul escapes the body, the god uses the rainbow as a ladder reaching the Moon. From there the soul is transformed into rain that will fall on land and reincarnate.

The rainbow has long been associated with the occult. "Rainbow witches" identify with the "joie de vivre path," the creative enjoyment of life's bounties. The seven colors of the rainbow are reflected in various objects useful for sacraments, especially goddess rites – prisms, crystals, rainbow quartzes, opals, moonstones, white pearls, abalone shells. These also provide wish charms, often used for prosperity, and to help ease disappointment, especially for children.

Rainwater: Rain is life, and purified rainwater adds its essence to a variety of sacraments. For many cultures the process begins with a dance to invoke rain. Even the Brits, who sometimes have more rain than they know what to do with, have their own system for  more. Their device is the rural Green Man, usually depicted as a horned god peeping out of foliage and believed to provide lush meadows. Rain dances are crucial, especially in arid regions. For our own sacramental purposes, we make use of an ancient pagan system in preparing the water.

In a large crystal bowl or jar holding seashells or gemstones, set the container in the rain until full. Strain through a coffee filter or cheesecloth and transfer water to smaller  clean bottles with caps. Do not drink the water. Label the jars with the date, Moon phase, astrological sign. Store the bottles on an altar or special place until the next full moon. At that time place nine white candles in the dry bowl you used for collecting and fill one-third with coarse salt. Place candles to form a circle around the jars on the altar. Light the candles and burn a smudge stick and frankincense or other incense. Wave the smoke over the bottles with a feather and say, Full Moon Goddess anoint this rain, power and goodness it shall gain.

If you choose, add gemstones or tiny seashells to the water as well as the herb rue to increase the power. Use the rainwater in working spells, blessings, cleaning special tools and sprinkling around the edges of magic circles.

Rhodonite: A pink stone with black veining, usually found as a massive single stone; sometimes smaller crystals are found, rare and more valuable. The name "rhodonite" is derived from the Greek "rhodon," meaning, "rose." Typically this stone is found in Europe and Australia, but sometimes emerges elsewhere in the world. Rhodonite is a stone of love and often this sentiment is manifest in self actualization. This earthly gem helps to stabilize emotions, which provides confidence and allows wearers to achieve their full potential. Often helpful in friendships, relationships and negotiating, rhodonite would do well placed in a desk drawer or near the threshold of your front door.

Rosemary: Rosemary (dew of the sea) is an amuletic herb used in myriad charms to draw, protect, purify, and encourage love. It's believed to increase mental agility, combat insomnia, and placing rosemary under your pillow is said to ward off bad dreams. It's also hung on doors to keep thieves out. Medieval brides wore rosemary at their weddings because of its association with love and fidelity. Rosemary is associated with the element of fire and with the Sun.

ROSEMARY
Rosmarinus
officinalis

Roses: Everyone recognizes the obvious universal connection to love, beauty and romance, but this flower has special significance to Witches and pagans. The rose is an ancient goddess symbol specific to deities of love and beauty – Roman Venus and her Greek counterpart, Aphrodite, among others. In magic the number five is associated with these goddesses,

Rose, from Macer's Viribus Herbarum, *Naples, 1477*

perhaps also connecting with the five petals of the rose. This also reflects the appeal to pagans, since the symbol is a parallel to the pentagram or pentacle.

The Rosicrucians adapted the Rose Cross as their symbol, but their emblem featured twenty-two petals, denoting the number of Cabbalistic paths on the Tree of Life. Much of the symbolism from pre-Christian cultures was adapted for the newer religion, and so with the rose. Once held as a goddess symbol, the rose became associated with the Virgin Mary. The flower also inspired the name of rosary beads, long predated by the prayer beads of various cultures. The flower's uses in aromatherapy are well known; the fragrance is uplifting to those with a heavy heart.

The rose plays a stellar role in love magic. A strand of fragrant beads made from powdered rose petals, orrisroot, with rose absolute adding to the scent, is a charming gift of love. These beads should be made

and strung in numbers which equal the number five, such as fourteen, twenty-three, forty-one, etc. Once done, meditate and charge the strands with your intent. When honoring the goddess or asking that a boon be granted, the rose is a favorite flower to grace an altar.

Rowan: Its red berries strung on red thread is a good luck charm. A rowan tree growing close to the house protects it and its inhabitants. Carrying this wood is believed to increase psychic ability, which may be why rowan is considered an excellent choice for divining rods.

ROWAN
Sorbus aucuparia

Ruby: The most valued gem among the Hindus, the ruby is considered the king of gemstones. It is a stone of Mars and protects warriors in battle, bestowing a sense of invulnerability upon them. This stone is thought to bring wealth and loyalty, preserve the physical and mental health of the wearer, offer protection from all negative influences, banish melancholy, warm the body, and surround the wearer with an aura of beauty. Some believe that rubies actually darken when danger is approaching.

A ruby set in French Gothic design

Rue: Rue has a strong history of magic in witchcraft. It was a favored herb of the high priests in ancient times. Arabs cherish it because it is the only herb known to be blessed by Mohammed. In Iraq, the sprigs are eaten to overcome fears

RUE
Ruta graveolens

and inspire bravery. Rue was worn to protect against the plague and other illnesses. The scent of the fresh, crushed leaves is thought to drive away envious thoughts, and when added to a bath rue eradicates spells and hexes placed on you. A sprig of rue can be dipped into water and used to sprinkle an area for magical purification. Hang a sprig to protect your home against all kinds of evil.

Runes: Form of writing most closely associated with ancient northern Germany, Old Norse, and Scandinavian cultures. Runes are composed primarily of straight line segments because originally the symbols were carved into stone or wood. Since the advent of paper, some of the forms have been modified to incorporate curves. Other than their use as an alphabet, the runic symbols express a wide variety of meanings and are used in magical work and divination. The symbol itself not only stood for but became the object in magical work.

Sun   Good Luck   Water   Love

Comfort   Victory   Possession   Mankind

Sage: Sage is under the dominion of Jupiter and is thought to exert an overall beneficial effect on the spirit and body. The plant was used by many ancient cultures for its cleansing and protective force and was reputed to promote longevity. It is primarily used for healing and prosperity. Sage is burned in the home to eradicate any lingering negativity or evil, and to provide

SAGE
Salvia officinalis

protection from these things. It's also believed to suppress unnatural sexual desires and to restore virility. This herb is said to grow best in the gardens of the wise.

ST. JOHN'S WORT
*Hypericum
perforatum*

St. John's Wort: This sacred herb of the Celtic tribes has recently come to prominence for its healing virtues, though for centuries it has been believed to protect against evil thoughts. It is closely associated with Midsummer Eve, when it was traditionally collected and passed through the smoke of festival fires. The herb was thought to protect witches and was frequently used in magic. It is burned to dispel evil and negativity, and hung in the home to guard against harm and loss and to prevent the spells of others from entering. The herb is worn for success in battles of any kind, as it instills courage and strengthens the will. Hanging the herb over your bed banishes nightmares, while sleeping with a sprig under your pillow is rumored to bring dreams of a future love.

Salt: The familiar seasoning in every kitchen has long held significant roles in the most solemn of rituals. People in many cultures believe that salt symbolizes purity. Greek worshippers consecrated it on their altars, and offerings at the Temple of Solomon included salt. Jews still dip bread into salt on the Sabbath to commemorate that ancient usage. The snowy substance turns up often in both the Old and New Testaments, and salt sealed covenants of all kinds, the origin of the word "salvation." Lot's wife was turned into a pillar of salt. In the Catholic Church, salt appears in a variety of purifying rituals. Jesus called his disciples, "the salt of the earth." In Da Vinci's famous painting, "The Last Supper," Judas has just spilled a bowl of salt – an evil omen. Since ancient times spilling salt requires throwing a pinch over your shoulder to ward off any hovering demons. Buddhist tradition calls for the same observance to ward off bad spirits before entering a house observing a funeral. Shinto believers also use salt for purifying a site. Sumo wrestlers throw a handful of salt into the ring before they enter, again to ward off unwelcome invisible visitors. In 1933 the previous Dalai Lama was entombed sitting up to his neck in salt. The substance played a potent role in Mahatma Gandhi's liberation efforts. He led a famous walk to the sea, gathering tax-free salt for the poor. Still today salt may be used as a purifying sacrament, and a gift of salt portends good luck.

Sapphire: This gem, sacred to the Greek god Zeus, protects against envy or any other source that creates evil intent, and offers prophetic wisdom to the wearer. The deep blue color of this stone was likened to the pure sky and it became regarded as a symbol of purity, making it popular in ecclesiastical rings. Sapphires promote love and fidelity, banish fraud, and heighten psychic ability. They were considered an antidote against poison and were also used to cure eye ailments, purify the blood, and strengthen the heart. Star sapphires are thought to be extremely potent, so much so that they exert a benign influence on their first wearer even when ownership has passed on to another.

Brooch of gold with a sapphire inlaid, French, 1850

Scapular: Two small squares of cloth joined by strings to hang over the shoulders. The squares are adorned with Roman Catholic images and are worn as a symbol of devotion, meant to secure eternal life and to help the wearer avoid eternal fire. The squares, which must be blessed by a

priest, are worn under the clothes and protect the chest and back. The custom derives from Roman times when Jupiter and Juno or other gods appeared on the squares, though it is still in practice during the 21st century by devout Roman Catholics.

Scarab: The most common ancient Egyptian amulet rivaling the ankh as a protective and good luck force. The name scarab comes from the fact that their shape resembles that of the dung beetle, or *Scarabaeus sacer*. The beetle was seen in ancient Egypt as the embodiment of the creator god because it was thought to perform self-creation. The scarab symbolizes creation and rebirth; it signifies the life force.

Royal seal of Menkure, Fourth Dynasty

Sea shells: Water, the sea, and shells are feminine in nature. As an amulet or charm, sea shells are anointed with perfumed oil and with proper ceremony given to young women. Shells are considered symbols of protection and are also used in love spells.

Shen: The potent symbol of eternity to the ancient Egyptians represents the sun's orbit. The sacred shen figures prominently in the tombs of the pharaohs to ensure a promise of everlasting life, or for as long as the sun revolves in the sky. A dramatic golden image from the tomb of Amenhotep II depicts the

goddess Isis. Her hand rests lightly on the shen as she kneels upon an emblem of gold to assure the dead king of endless life. In the form of an amulet to be worn or carried, the shen was most often made of lapis lazuli or carnelian and adorned with gold, for the precious metal was strongly associated with the symbol and its concept.

Sodalite: A deep blue mineral often seen with white streaks or markings of calcite. Discovered in Greenland in 1806,

sodalite is one of the minerals found in the sought-after semi-precious stone lapis lazuli. Today Canada is the world's largest supplier of sodalite. This most beautiful stone will fluoresce under ultraviolet light. Darkness will also restore its brilliance, also accelerated by ultraviolet light. Sodalite inspires thoughts as deep as its color and encourages understanding through higher thinking. The stone is excellent for the seeker of wisdom, calming its wearer and promoting deep meditation leading to a balance of thought and spirit.

Tarragon: The Latin name of this herb of Mars means "little dragon of Artemis," and tarragon is believed to instill its wearer with the bravery attributed to the goddess of the hunt. It is also used as a shield against trouble. Carry some with you when you anticipate hostility or when facing any quest requiring confidence and good judgement.

TARRAGON
Artemisia
dracunculus

Tattva: The tattva is a Hindu system used to categorize the elements. In Sanskrit, tattva or tattwa means "reality" or "principle. Many schools of Hindu thought treat the tattva as an aspect of reality. As the physical elements in the West are thought to be the building blocks of our world, in the East tattva are seen in infinite combination as the basis of all life experience.

> Blue circle – *Vayu* – the element of air
> Red triangle – *Tejas* – the element of fire
> Yellow square – *Prithivi* – the element of earth
> Silver crescent – Apas – the element of water

Tau Cross: Pre-Christian protective amulet, known as a symbol of life. The Israelites used this symbol to mark the righteous, protecting them from destruction. It is also called St. Anthony's Cross. He was the first monk and established the idea of solitary life with spiritual dedication. St. Anthony departed from his village, lived as a hermit, and then was joined by other like-minded souls. From their example, the tradition of monasteries arose.

Tet: Ancient Egyptian symbol of stability. It's believed to represent the tree trunk in which Isis hid the body of her deceased husband Osiris, god of the dead. The tet is placed with mummies to lend strength to their backbones and give them power to reconstitute their bodies. Also called the *djed*.

Tetragrammaton: A talisman of the Cabala, this is a triangle within which the four Hebrew letters that make up the name of God are written. The tetragrammaton represents the creation of the universe, the power of fours in the universe (the four elements, the four seasons, the four direction points, etc.), and mathematically manifests the seventy-two powers of the Great Name of God. This symbol was later widely used in European ceremonial magic. *See Powers of the Tetragrammaton, p. 148.*

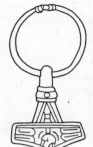

Thor's Hammer: A small, usually silver, protection amulet used by early Vikings to bestow upon the wearer the strength of Thor, god of thunder. The amulet represents masculinity and vengeance, and offers protection from lightning, fire, and other calamities.

Thyme: This herb of Venus figures in many love charms, including those used to restore vitality to a fading romance. Place thyme in your pillowcase to bring dreams of the future and repel nightmares. Burn it to purge a room of evil influences. Wild thyme rather than the tame garden kind is preferred for magical use.

THYME
Thymus vulgaris

Tiger-eye: Tiger-eye or tiger's eye is a variety of quartz with iron oxide providing gold stripes. The stone appears as an "eye" to the beholder, set in deep brown with blue asbestos lending a fibrous sheen. Most tiger-eye is found as large slabs in South Africa. In many cultures tiger-eye has long been associated with wealth, abundance and the earthy attributes of stability and health. The stone is also renowned for its use in protection, especially against the evil eye. Special sight, clairvoyance and psychic gifts of the third eye are said to be gifted to those who carry this stone in their pockets.

Tonka Bean: This fragrant seed, with an aroma similar to vanilla, is found in the Guianas and is popular as an amulet in the West Indies and Caribbean. It is used in love and protection charms, and is believed to be particularly powerful when tied to a cross.

Topaz: This gem of the Sun is believed to bestow fearlessness and wisdom upon its wearer. Among its many virtues, topaz is said to offer protection against sorcery, cure madness, and calm anger and other emotional excesses. The powers of topaz were once believed to increase and decrease along with the phases of the Moon.

Torch: A symbol of light and protection against the powers of darkness. The torch is carried by a leader, a "torch bearer," to show the way, sometimes an official offering inspiration. Its sacred ritual use in various cultures is ancient. The Greeks revered fire, believing it was stolen from Zeus and given to humankind by Prometheus. *Dadouches*, the Greek

term for 'torch bearer,' was the title of a celebrant officiating at the Eleusinian mysteries. A torch was used in relays from the most ancient Olympics and still appears similarly in modern contests. (Beijing's Summer Olympics of a few years ago provided a torch extravaganza.) In Greece torches burned during the games. Mirrors were used to focus flames onto torches that burned perpetually in front of temples. In Rome the Vestal Virgins made use of torches to

maintain the *ignis inextinctus*, the sacred fire in the Temple of Vesta.

The ancient Arabs honored Atthar, the goddess of enlightenment, known as the "Torch of the Gods." At the New Year Tibetans celebrate Guduo, a festival of "expelling the ghost" believed to keep the site safe from bad spirits for the year. In monasteries and homes after a traditional dinner of barley soup a man lights a torch and leads others from room to room, chanting, "Take all the bad luck away and never return, get out, get out." In less formal ceremonials, torches turn up for various purposes, useful for bonfires, especially at Beltane.

Tree Cones: These are often used in fertility charms, especially the tiny cones of the hemlock tree that are strung on red thread and worn by women desiring children. Pine cones are widely used in fertility charms and were highly valued by the cult of Venus.

Triskelion: Its name derives from the Greek word for three-legged. A triskelion has three branches or three running legs radiating from a center, and has appeared in cultures all over the world. It is an amulet of protection and good luck.

Turquoise: This stone has a long-standing reputation for offering protection from injuries during falls, especially falls from horseback. Attached to the bridle as an amulet, it also protects horses. Turquoise is highly prized by Native Americans. When affixed to a weapon, turquoise was thought to give hunters and warriors unerring aim. This stone is used in love charms, and when given as a gift to a lover is supposed to retain its color as long as the love lasts. Turquoise is said to change color as a reflection of the health of its wearer.

Unakite: Found in South Carolina, unakite is named for the town where it was discovered. Its dual colors of green and pink usually have a mottled pattern and are made primarily of epidote. Considering unakite, emotions become the key word. The two contrasting colors often represent balance and can be used for matters relating to such concerns. Unakite is a "strong" stone used for healing troubled emotions and feelings of separation or abandonment. Depression and deception can be thwarted through proper use of this gemstone. It is also known to facilitate healthy pregnancy and safe childbirth.

Ushabti: These are tiny figurines placed in ancient Egyptian tombs representing servants who would perform tasks for and protect the deceased in the afterlife. Their very name means "respondent." They are sometimes referred to as *ushebtiu*.

Utchat: The Eye of Horus is one of the most common Egyptian amulets. It gives its wearer health, strength, protection, and the vigor of the life-giving sun. There are two versions of this symbol – one facing right, one facing left – and these are sometimes called the Eye of Ra and the Eye of Osiris, respectively, with one representing the Sun, the other the Moon. The *Book of the Dead* says these amulets should be made from lapis lazuli, though many are made from other gemstones or metals. The utchat was placed with the deceased or painted on an object for protection.

VALERIAN
Valeriana officinalis

Valerian: Its Latin name, *Valeriana officinalis*, means powerful and of medicinal value. An herb of Mercury, it features clusters of small fragrant pink flowers used in love charms to promote harmony. Its foul-smelling root (vandal root) is widely used as a nerve remedy and stimulating tonic, though large doses cause headache and mental agitation. Cats are very drawn to its unpleasant odor.

Veils: The veil symbolizes a barrier separating ordinary consciousness from the spirit world, sometimes defined as a curtain between microcosm and macrocosm. Varying transparencies exist and sometimes we get glimpses beyond, as when we have an uneasy feeling that a friend is in danger. The phenomenon is called the "Veil of Paroketh" in the Qabalah, the "veil between worlds." Widows wear veils to proclaim their "crone status" and as protection from the ghost world where their

Nineteenth century veiled Egyptian female

115

deceased husbands dwell. Brides wear white veils that will be lifted at the altar, signifying the ancient view that at this boundary they pass from a father's care to a husband's. Nunnery novices also wear white veils as brides of Christ that, according to St. Paul, represent not so much purity as "inviolable constancy."

Methods for transcending the boundary, "tearing the veil" are in place from a variety of systems. For use in magic, colors of veils represent the life stages – white for the maiden, red for the mother, black or deep purple for the older woman. Assume a sheer veil of the appropriate color, light candles and incense, and seat yourself before a mirror at an altar decorated with flowers, fruit or seeds. Welcome whatever spirits you choose to invoke. Sit quietly until you are ready to lift the veil and say, "It is done."

VERVAIN
Verbena officinalis

Vervain: Most sacred of all herbs of witchcraft, this cure-all was extensively used by the Druids, particularly in divination. It is an herb of Venus, and so is used in many love charms. Roman brides collected vervain and wore wreaths of it at their weddings. Though widely used in witchcraft, it was also deemed capable of "hindering witches of their will."

Vèvè: This is a magical design representing astral forces and is an integral part of Voodoo ritual. The design can be drawn on a piece of heavy paper and carried as a charm for any purpose associated with the divine *loa*, or sacred spirit it represents.

Vèvè of Erzulie, goddess of love

WILLOW
Salix alba

Willow: The willow is associated with several gods. In Egypt, it was sacred to Osiris because the tree was believed to have sheltered his body after he was killed, and then later his soul sat in a willow in the form of a bird. The Greek goddess Hera was born under a willow, and the touch of a willow branch brought Orpheus supernatural eloquence. Willow groves are sacred to Hecate, goddess of witchcraft. Willow is used in spells to dismiss love and turn passion to friendship. Pussy willow is used in love charms as protection against evil, and its wands are used in divination.

Witch Balls: These are protective amulets made of colorful blown glass and hung in windows to safeguard against the Evil Eye. The weblike strands of glass inside the ball were thought to trap evil spirits before they entered the home.

Wormwood: This is an herb of Mars, though it is said that the goddess Artemis found this silvery plant so beneficial that she chose it for her own. It is used in a love charm

WORMWOOD
Artemisia absinthium

with marigold, marjoram, and thyme to provoke dreams of a future mate. It has been widely used as a vermifuge to keep away moths and insects. The potent liquor absinthe is made from wormwood extracts. In a Mexican fete honoring Huixtocihuatl, goddess of salt, women linked together with flowering boughs wear garlands of wormwood on their heads and perform a dance invoking the goddess.

X-shaped Cross: This symbol has a bewildering number of meanings: crossroads, Christ as in Xmas, wrong on an exam, an unknown quantity, signature for the illiterate, multiplication symbol, railway crossing sign, and a kiss. In Roman Catholic tradition, the equal-armed cross is the emblem of St. Andrew. In witchcraft a willow rod, or wishing wand, is inscribed on the handle with  four dots and three crosses • x • x • x • and the dots are spaced to fit your fingertips when you hold the wand. Close your eyes, cross your fingers to ensure a wish comes true.

Yarrow: Considered an herb of Venus, *Achillea millefolium* is actually named for the Greek hero Achilles, the first to use its healing properties on himself and his soldiers for battle wounds. Yarrow, a sacred witch plant from earliest time is used in divination and fortune-telling. When eaten by a couple at their wedding, it ensured seven years of love. Sleep with yarrow under your pillow to dream of your true love.

Achilles

Yin and Yang: The ancient Chinese sign defines two great opposing forces of the universe. Black side, yin, is said to represent female, passive, evil; white side, yang, is male, active, and goodness. Each side has a dot of the opposing color to show that each contains a seed of the other. The two opposing forces form one harmonious whole. The symbol shows the balance of opposing forces in nature; one cannot exist without the other.

Zodiac Symbols: No one can say where or when the graphic symbols of the signs of the zodiac originated. Oddly, they bear little if any resemblance to the constellations they identify. By the 16th century, the set of twelve symbols were firmly established throughout Europe and astrologers of all nations use them to the present day. Individual symbols cast in metal are often worn as amulets by those who strongly believe in the power of their own sign. Ancient astrological themes defined the quality and shaped the character of the twelve divisions of the zodiac circle.

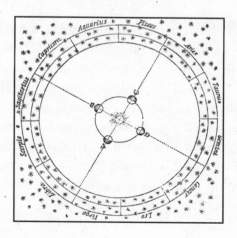

ARIES
March 21 – April 20

Traditions old at the time of Ptolemy place Aries under the rulership of Mars – planet of vigor, violence, and aggression. The Ram is the first of the four cardinal signs because its advent marks the beginning of spring and the start of a new year. It isn't surprising to find force and initiative attributed to those born under Aries. The leader of the heavenly flock is diurnal (the Day House of Mars), masculine, positive, active, of a choleric humor, hot, dry, and a member of the fiery trine.

TAURUS
April 21 – May 21

Nocturnal, feminine, negative, passive, calm, cold, dry, and earthy are qualities assigned to Taurus by the ancient astrologers. The second sign of the zodiac reigns during the height of the spring season and for this reason is designated as fixed, indicating stability. Key words such as patient, placid, and reliable have been used for more than two thousand years to describe the Bull's nature. Sensuality, creativity, and an appreciation of beauty are gifts of the love goddess, for Taurus occupies the Night House of Venus.

GEMINI
May 22 – June 21

The Day House of Mercury belongs to the Twins. Nimble mind, quick tongue, and sharp wit are bestowed by the Messenger – swiftest of planets and god of communication and curiosity. As Gemini is overhead when spring gives way to summer, it is called mutable, signifying a time of change. Diurnal, masculine, positive, active, cheerful, hot, moist, and first of the three air signs are the classical definitions. These qualities give rise to the restless, changeable, unpredictable, chameleonlike character assigned to Gemini. As the first human and dual image of the zodiac, the Twins receive credit for family devotion along with charges of duplicity.

Children of the planet Mercury

CANCER
June 22 – July 23

Cancer alone owns the Mansion of the Moon. All the ancient assigned qualities of this sign reflect the influence of the ruler of the night – nocturnal, feminine, negative, passive, cold, moist, melancholy, and cardinal of the three water signs. These qualities easily interpret as the intuitive, emotional, mysterious and compelling personality defined for the Crab. Restlessness and a need to be on the move come from the Moon as well as being characteristic of a cardinal sign. Cancer's arrival coincides with the beginning of the summer season. The Moon, symbol of magic, madness, and love, is said to guide the destiny of all those born under her sway.

Luna

LEO
July 24 – August 23

Throughout antiquity the astrological sign of Leo was ever identified with the Sun. Sole occupant of the House of the Sun, it is said that the Lion will always advance in life for his ruler never retrogrades. As the fixed sign of the fiery trine, Leo presides over the height of summer matching the maximum heat and light of the Sun. Choleric (fiery) humor, masculine gender, positive and active nature, hot, dry, and naturally diurnal describe the powerful, vital, dominating, and extremely creative character astrologically defined for Leo.

VIRGO
August 24 – September 23

The Virgin of classical myth is Proserpine, daughter of Ceres, the Earth Mother. The maiden's abduction marks the end of growing season and celebrates harvest. Although a mutable sign, one that spans two seasons, the Virgin is defined as adaptable rather than unstable, for she belongs to the steadfast trine of earth. Nocturnal, feminine, negative, passive, cold, dry, and calm describe the maiden who must return each year to the underworld kingdom. Virgo owns the Night Mansion of Mercury and his quicksilver gifts lend mental agility and deftness.

LIBRA
September 24 – October 23

At the autumnal equinox the days and nights on Earth are of equal length. A cardinal sign occurring at this time of year is called the Balance. Some early zodiacs depict a man holding the scales in perfect balance, but since the Middle Ages Libra's image has been scales alone – often wildly out of balance. Ancient astrologers call Libra masculine, positive, active, hot, moist, and one of the airy triplicity. These qualities do not suggest composure nor does Libra's placement in the Day House of Venus. In classical times the influence of Venus over an air sign was considered a mixed blessing, for instinctive pleasure can become self-indulgence.

SCORPIO
October 24 – November 22

The ancients placed Scorpio in the Night Mansion of Mars. When Pluto was discovered in 1930, modern astrologers asserted that the sign of death and regeneration belonged to the dread Lord of the Underworld. The mystery still surrounding Pluto and its forces allows Scorpio to continue possessing Martian traits of courage, discipline, and self-control. Nocturnal and feminine, Scorpio is the fixed sign of the watery trine. Cold, moist, negative, passive, melancholy qualities form the intense, secretive, passionate, and relentless nature attributed to Scorpio. An alternative symbol for mid-autumn's sign is the eagle.

SAGITTARIUS
November 23 – December 21

Babylonian inscriptions from the dawn of history refer to this sign as the Strong One. Power, magnanimity, and mercy are appropriate traits for those who dwell in the Day House of Jupiter, ruler of the gods. As the only figure of the zodiac which combines man and beast, the Archer bestows remarkable understanding of and affinity for all living creatures. Classical astrologers considered Sagittarius to be masculine, diurnal, positive, active, hot, dry, choleric, and belonging to the fiery trine. But mutability lends an elusive inconstancy to an otherwise noble character, because the Archer rules as autumn gives way to winter.

CAPRICORN
December 22 – January 20

The Sea-Goat lives in the Night House of Saturn and it is from this god's baleful influence that many of the sign's negative aspects derive. Saturn is the Roman equivalent of the Greek god Cronos, who destroyed his father Uranus and devoured his own children. The most remote planet in Ptolemy's day, Saturn was likened to the exiled Cronos when Zeus came to power. It fell to the distant Saturn to rule the coldest time of the year. Capricorn's qualities are nocturnal, feminine, negative, passive, phlegmatic, cold, dry, and of the earth trine. A cardinal sign because it heralds winter, the goat is endowed with authority, determination, and inventiveness.

AQUARIUS
January 21 – February 19

In 1781 a new planet was discovered and named Uranus for the Greek sky-god, father and originator of all living things. Aquarius, the Water Bearer, belonged to the Day House of Saturn until 19th-century astrologers decided that the house of Uranus was a more appropriate lodging. The fixed sign of the airy triplicity is defined as masculine, diurnal, positive, active, cheerful, hot, and moist. These characteristics agree with the humanitarian image of Aquarius, the single mortal of the zodiac, who brings comfort and healing to Earth. And it suits the explosive, inventive, sensitive, and perceptive nature ascribed to the sky-god.

PISCES
February 20 – March 20

Emotional, mystic, yielding, ever-changing are descriptions derived from the classical astrologers' assessment of Pisces. The mutable sign of the watery trine signaling winter's end is defined as nocturnal, feminine, negative, passive, cold, moist, and melancholy. For many centuries the Fishes swam in the Night House of Jupiter, and that god's quality of might and majesty added strength and stability to the sign. When the planet Neptune was discovered in 1795 and astrologers transferred Pisces to the rulership of the god of the sea, the dreaminess and impressionability of the sign's interpretation increased.

THREE WAYS TO BLESS A CHARM

ESSENTIALLY it is the quality of mind and imagination that can infuse an appropriate object with magical power. The ceremonial magician enhances consciousness by means of fasting, chastity, and cleanliness. The materials assembled for the ritual must be new. Timing of the operation, placement of planets, venue, and vestments are all vital considerations. Such elaborate preparations are believed to intensify the experience and secure a successful outcome. Or as witches say, "We will better when we're in the mood for willing." Three examples of typical blessing rites follow.

 NCIENT

ONE OF THE OLDEST texts describing a ceremony to bless an amulet is taken from a Greek magical papyrus written during the early centuries of the Common Era. The translation was published by the Cambridge Antiquarian Society of England in 1852 under the title of *Fragment of a Graeco-Egyptian Work upon Magic*. It has been slightly edited for clarity:

Blessing Ceremony   Greek, 470 B.C.E.

Ceremony of the Beetle

THE SCARAB shall be carved out of a precious emerald; bore it and pass a gold wire through it, and beneath the beetle carve the holy Isis, and having consecrated it as written below, use it. The proper days of the consecration are the 7th, 9th, 10th, 12th, 14th, 16th, 21st, 24th, and 25th, from the beginning of the month of Thoth (29 August); on other days abstain.

Take the sculptured beetle and place it on a paper tablet, and under the tablet there shall be a pure linen cloth; under it put some olive wood, and set on the middle of the tablet a small censer wherein myrrh and kyphi (see note) shall be offered. And have at hand a small vessel of chrysolite into which ointment of lilies, or myrrh, or cinnamon, shall be put, and take the scarab and lay it in the ointment, having first made it pure and clean, and offer it up in the smoke of the censer. Leave the amulet in the chrysolite vessel for three days.

Note: Several arcane references may require explanation. Kyphi incense used in the ceremony was favored by the priesthood of ancient Egypt. According to later sources, kyphi consisted of juniper berries, myrrh gum, orris root, cardamom seeds, broom, sweet rush, honey, wine, raisins, frankincense and other resins. Chrysolite is a volcanic green stone found throughout the world. Translucent or transparent, its color varies from yellow-green to deep olive and in its clear form provides the gemstones of peridot and olivine. Unction is another word for ointment or oil, especially used as a classical term for spiritual anointing.

At the celebration let there lie near at hand some pure loaves, and such fruit as are in season, and having made another offering upon vine sticks, take the scarab out of the ointment, and anoint thyself with the unction from it. Thou shalt anoint thyself early in the morning, and turning toward the east shalt pronounce these words:

Hail to thee, O Thoth,
inventor and founder of medicines and letters;
Come to me, thou that art under the earth,
rise up to me, thou great spirit.

Thoth, tomb of Ramses II   14th–13th century B.C.E.

The Domain of Venus   Hans Sebald Beham, 1530

 EDIEVAL

CEREMONIAL MAGIC is a curious mix of archaic lore, astrological principles, Hebrew mysticism, and Roman Catholic rites. Rules of magic for spiritual work are contained in a series of *grimoires*, esoteric textbooks written in various European languages during the Middle Ages. The *Key of Solomon* may be the oldest, for a Greek version in manuscript form dates to the late 12th century. By the 16th century, the invention of printing spawned a succession of volumes devoted to ceremonial magic. To perform as simple an operation as blessing a talisman required extraordinary diligence. The following ritual is based on many themes culled from the medieval texts:

Venus pentacle from The Greater Key of Solomon, *16th-century manuscript*

To Consecrate a Love Talisman

♥LOVE BELONGS to the domain of Venus, planet of poetry, music, joy, and harmony. That planet's placement was the first consideration. A well-aspected Venus should be in the zodiac's sign of Pisces, in direct motion, for a retrograde Venus would undermine the operation. The Sun must be in either Taurus or Libra, the signs ruled by Venus. The rite would take place on Friday, the day of Venus, and within the hours when that planet's power is strongest: midnight to 1 a.m., 7 to 8 a.m., 2 to 3 p.m., 9 to 10 p.m.

Early magical manuals decreed that the talisman chosen and all objects used to bless it must be new and never before used for any purpose. This strict rule extended to candles made from wax produced by bees for the first time. A simplification proposed by the *Grimorium Verum* (a French text dated 1517, but probably an 18th-century work) was a process of aspersion, an archaic term meaning to sprinkle with holy water, and fumigation. *True Black Magic* published in Rome in 1750 describes the instrument of aspersion: "And the aspergillum is a bouquet of vervain, periwinkle, sage, mint, valerian, ash, basil, and rosemary forming a brush. Fit it with a handle of virgin hazel, three palms in length, and dip it in a glazed earthen pot filled with fresh spring water. Sprinkle over all. This device may be used on any occasion with perfect assurance that all phantoms will be expelled from every place which shall be sprinkled thereby and so exorcised."

Fumigation was accomplished by "taking a new coal which has not been kindled, setting it alight, and while it is still black, exorcising it, saying: "I exorcise thee, O creature of Fire, by Him Who hath made all things!" The fumes of incense placed on the live coal pleasantly dispersed any lingering evil spirits. A love talisman would be consecrated with scents most pleasing to Venus: aloes wood, ambergris, sandalwood, musk, rose, myrtle, and resins of galbanum and storax.

The talisman might be the symbol of Venus inscribed on parchment in black ink. A precious gem or a scrap of sea-glass engraved with an appropriate image must be green, the color of Venus. A square of duly incised and highly polished copper was another possibility, for copper is the metal associated with Venus.

The magician prepared with a period of fasting, chastity, and three hours of silence prior to the rite. A ritual bath and the donning of vestments followed. The 16th-century Italian *Grimoire of Honorius* advised a long surplice of white linen and bare feet as proper attire.

In a room reserved for magical work a sacred circle was defined by a nine-foot silk cord. Within the circle the purified objects were assembled: a small wooden table to serve as an altar covered by a white linen cloth, two white candles in glass holders, an incense burner to hold a fiery coal, incense, and the talisman. The candles were positioned to mark north on the left, south on the right, for the magician faced east in the performance of the rite. The room was darkened, candles lit, incense ignited, and the talisman was held aloft as prayers to Venus and her planetary angel Anael were recited. After the invocation, the magician asked that the talisman be blessed for his use and benefit. The talisman was left on the altar and not touched until the next day.

MODERN

ANOTHER WAY to bless a charm comes from a Book of Shadows kept by New England witch Katherine Irena Anderson during the early decades of the 20th century. While its practices are contemporary, they doubtless derive from ancient rituals handed down from generation to generation.

To Sanctify a Charm

While the Moon wanes, contrive to secretly burn a block of myrrh on a live coal. Sprinkle well with the dried crumbled herbs of rosemary and thyme. Pass the object to be purified through the rising smoke of the incense until you feel it is quite free of any previous emanations. Wrap the charm in a square of pure linen and hide it away in a safe place.

At Dark-of-the-Moon and at the midnight hour, place the charm in the center of a triangle of white paper in a room lit only by a single white candle. Visualize a circle connecting the points of the triangle and concentrate with all the intensity at your command on the quality you wish to impart to the charm. Raise the candle and with it form a clockwise circle around the triangle three times. Take care to complete the final circle at the point where the first began. Stare fixedly at the charm. The moment will come when you will reach out and hold the amulet in your hand. Snuff out the candle and in the darkness feel the power of the spirit force brought into being. Address the charm with these words:

> *I greet thee, spirit, ye who dwell within.*
> *Be my shield against all evil and ill chance*
> *that may befall my body and soul in time to*
> *come. So be it. I place my sacred trust in thee.*

CHARTS AND CORRESPONDENCES

OCCULT traditions arise regarding all manner of things: names, numbers, the passage of time, elements, creatures, products of the earth, and astrological patterns in the sky above. Such principles were established by the blending of many cultures in the ancient world and so provide a rich source of magical themes. To dismiss all arcane thought as mere superstition denies an instinctive quality existing in nature itself. Whatever produces a feeling of optimism, security, and confidence is worthy of attention. Here you will find a variety of correlations that clearly reflect a sound and sensible attitude to life and its gifts.

PYTHAGOREAN NUMBERS

The 6th-century B.C.E. philosopher Pythagoras taught that each number has its own peculiar character, virtue, and properties.

1 One is the number of essence. It is the symbol of identity, of equality, of existence, of conservation, and of general harmony. Having no parts, a single unit announces order, peace, and tranquillity, which are founded on unity of sentiments; consequently, one is a good principle.

2 The number two, the origin of contrasts, is the symbol of diversity and inequality, of division and separation. Two is accordingly an evil principle, a number of bad augury, characterizing disorder, confusion, and change.

3 Three is the first of unequals; it is the number containing the most sublime mysteries, for every thing is composed of three substances. It represents divinity, the soul of the world, the spirit of man. It is meditation, atonement, completeness – beginning, middle, end.

4 Four, the first mathematical power, is also one of the chief elements. It represents the generating virtue, whence come all combinations; it is the most perfect of numbers; it is the root of all things. Pythagoreans swear by the quaternary number, which gives the human soul its eternal nature.

5 The number five has a peculiar force in sacred expiations; it is every thing; it stops the power of poisons, and is redoubted by evil spirits.

6 Six is a fortunate number, the number of luck and chance. It derives its merit from the first sculptors having divided the face into six portions. According to the Chaldeans, the reason is, because the world was created in six days.

7 Seven is a number very powerful for good or for evil. It is the number of the entire cosmos. It belongs especially to sacred things.

8 The number eight is the first cube, that is to say, squared in all senses, as a die, proceeding from its base two, an even number; so is man four-square, or perfect.

9 The cube of three being nine, nine is regarded as the extent to which numbers would go, all others being embraced and revolving within it. Ten but recommences a fresh series capable of infinite expansion. Nine should be regarded as sacred.

– *From* Life of Pythagoras *by Iamblichus (c. 250 – c. 330)*

# AN OCCULT ALPHABET

IN 1801 Francis Barrett, English scholar of occult philosophy and the Cabala, published a curious volume called *The Magus*. Among the illustrations we find this occult alphabet. Its legend reads, "The Mysterious Characters of Letters deliver'd by Honorius call'd the Theban Alphabet." Honorius II, Pope from 1216 to 1227, sponsored a crusade to Egypt and was reputed to be a master magician. Several medieval *grimoires* (magical texts) are attributed to him.

Our English J, U and W had no equivalents in Middle Latin. Modern occultists use the symbols for I and V as substitutes for the missing letters. The final character has been translated as the Greek *alpha* and *omega*, the beginning and end.

A	B	C	D	E	F
G	H	I	K	L	M
N	O	P	Q	R	S
T	V	X	Y	Z	*alpha omega*

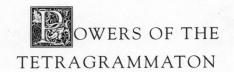

POWERS OF THE
TETRAGRAMMATON

Essence of the Infinite Beginning

HE = 5   VAU = 6   HE = 5   YOD = 10

The four letters of the Great Name I H V H (written from right to left in Hebrew) form the base of the Pythagorean Tetractys illustrated above. The seventy-two powers of the Name of Four Letters are manifested by the triangle in the manner outlined on the next page.

•					I			10		=	10
•		•			H	I		5+10		=	15
•	•		•		V	H	I	6+5+10		=	21
•	•	•	•	H	V	H	I	5+6+5+10		=	26
											72

Yod	*He*	*Vau*	*He*
Male	Female	Male	Female
East	West	South	North
Fire	Water	Air	Earth
Hot and Dry	Cold and Wet	Hot and Wet	Cold and Dry
The Sun	The Moon	The Sky	The Earth
Dawn	Twilight	Noon	Midnight
Spring	Autumn	Summer	Winter
Batons	Cups	Swords	Coins
Will	Insight	Mind	Body

Hermetic Tree of Knowledge

The Planetary Hours   Augsburg, 1490

PLANETARY DAYS AND HOURS

SUN	MOON	MARS	MERCURY	JUPITER	VENUS	SATURN
Sunday	*Monday*	*Tuesday*	*Wednesday*	*Thursday*	*Friday*	*Saturday*

PLANETARY DAYS were selected over two thousand years ago when the ancients named a day for each of the seven celestial bodies observed to move across the sky: the Sun, the Moon, and five planets visible to the naked eye. Unlike fixed constellations of stars, the planets (from the Greek word meaning "wandering") moved independently on separate courses. After the primary luminaries, the Sun and Moon, the Romans named the planets for gods exhibiting similar qualities. The red planet suited Mars, the fastest moving became Mercury, the largest and brightest was Jupiter, the most beautiful could only be Venus, and the most distant and forbidding was in accord with the character of Saturn.

Our English names of Sunday, Monday, and Saturday conform to the Latin equivalents, but the other four were inspired by Anglo-Saxon divinities: Tuesday honors Tiu, god of war; Wednesday belongs to Woden, the sky-father; Thursday is named for Thor, god of thunder; and Friday is Freya's day, goddess of love and beauty.

Albertus Magnus, the 13th-century Bavarian philosopher, first established the type of magical work governed by each heavenly body. Here is how the form has evolved:

SUN
Illumination, energy, action, hope,
self-expression, motivation

MOON
Enchantment, dreams, wishes, moods, plans, habits, ways

MARS
Growth, strength, health, defense,
sex life, matrimony, hostility

MERCURY
Wisdom, intelligence, opinion, fear, debt, nervous tension

JUPITER
Law, honor, expansion, humor, wealth,
adventure, bold quests

VENUS
Love, desire, harmony, constancy, friendship, unity, beauty

SATURN
Peace, divination, change, ambition,
progress, patience, loss

WHY THE planetary hours do not proceed in the same order as the days of the week is a mystery. Study the old German woodcut on page 150 and you'll be able to remember the proper sequence. There's Mars in full armor at twelve o'clock high and following him, the majestic Sun: next comes Venus holding her arrow of desire and after her, Mercury with his staff and serpent. The wistful Moon, old Saturn with his scythe, and vital Jupiter bearing a flowering bough complete the circle.

When clocks began to replace sundials and hourglasses as timekeepers, the system of planetary hours became more precise. It was the scholarly Peter of Abano who first used the clock rather than the ever-changing times of sunrise and sunset as his guide. He reckoned the planetary hours from midnight to midnight, each first hour ruled by the planet for which that day was named. The system Peter of Abano presented in *Magical Elements* is still in use today – seven centuries later.

Sunday – SUN

Midnight		Noon	
SUN	12 to 1 a.m.	JUPITER	12 to 1 p.m.
VENUS	1 to 2	MARS	1 to 2
MERCURY	2 to 3	SUN	2 to 3
MOON	3 to 4	VENUS	3 to 4
SATURN	4 to 5	MERCURY	4 to 5
JUPITER	5 to 6	MOON	5 to 6
MARS	6 to 7	SATURN	6 to 7
SUN	7 to 8	JUPITER	7 to 8
VENUS	8 to 9	MARS	8 to 9
MERCURY	9 to 10	SUN	9 to 10
MOON	10 to 11	VENUS	10 to 11
SATURN	11 to 12	MERCURY	11 to 12

Monday – MOON

Midnight		Noon	
MOON	12 to 1 a.m.	VENUS	12 to 1 p.m.
SATURN	1 to 2	MERCURY	1 to 2
JUPITER	2 to 3	MOON	2 to 3
MARS	3 to 4	SATURN	3 to 4
SUN	4 to 5	JUPITER	4 to 5
VENUS	5 to 6	MARS	5 to 6
MERCURY	6 to 7	SUN	6 to 7
MOON	7 to 8	VENUS	7 to 8
SATURN	8 to 9	MERCURY	8 to 9
JUPITER	9 to 10	MOON	9 to 10
MARS	10 to 11	SATURN	10 to 11
SUN	11 to 12	JUPITER	11 to 12

Tuesday – MARS

Midnight		Noon	
MARS	12 to 1 a.m.	SATURN	12 to 1 p.m.
SUN	1 to 2	JUPITER	1 to 2
VENUS	2 to 3	MARS	2 to 3
MERCURY	3 to 4	SUN	3 to 4
MOON	4 to 5	VENUS	4 to 5
SATURN	5 to 6	MERCURY	5 to 6
JUPITER	6 to 7	MOON	6 to 7
MARS	7 to 8	SATURN	7 to 8
SUN	8 to 9	JUPITER	8 to 9
VENU	9 to 10	MARS	9 to 10
MERCURY	10 to 11	SUN	10 to 11
MOON	11 to 12	VENUS	11 to 12

Wednesday – MERCURY

	Midnight		Noon
MERCURY	12 to 1 a.m.	SUN	12 to 1 p.m.
MOON	1 to 2	VENUS	1 to 2
SATURN	2 to 3	MERCURY	2 to 3
JUPITER	3 to 4	MOON	3 to 4
MARS	4 to 5	SATURN	4 to 5
SUN	5 to 6	JUPITER	5 to 6
VENUS	6 to 7	MARS	6 to 7
MERCURY	7 to 8	SUN	7 to 8
MOON	8 to 9	VENUS	8 to 9
SATURN	9 to 10	MERCURY	9 to 10
JUPITER	10 to 11	MOON	10 to 11
MARS	11 to 12	SATURN	11 to 12

Thursday – JUPITER

	Midnight		Noon
JUPITER	12 to 1 a.m.	MOON	12 to 1 p.m.
MARS	1 to 2	SATURN	1 to 2
SUN	2 to 3	JUPITER	2 to 3
VENUS	3 to 4	MARS	3 to 4
MERCURY	4 to 5	SUN	4 to 5
MOON	5 to 6	VENUS	5 to 6
SATURN	6 to 7	MERCURY	6 to 7
JUPITER	7 to 8	MOON	7 to 8
MARS	8 to 9	SATURN	8 to 9
SUN	9 to 10	JUPITER	9 to 10
VENUS	10 to 11	MARS	10 to 11
MERCURY	11 to 12	SUN	11 to 12

Friday – VENUS

Midnight		Noon	
VENUS	12 to 1 a.m.	MARS	12 to 1 p.m.
MERCURY	1 to 2	SUN	1 to 2
MOON	2 to 3	VENUS	2 to 3
SATURN	3 to 4	MERCURY	3 to 4
JUPITER	4 to 5	MOON	4 to 5
MARS	5 to 6	SATURN	5 to 6
SUN	6 to 7	JUPITER	6 to 7
VENUS	7 to 8	MARS	7 to 8
MERCURY	8 to 9	SUN	8 to 9
MOON	9 to 10	VENUS	9 to 10
SATURN	10 to 11	MERCURY	10 to 11
JUPITER	11 to 12	MOON	11 to 12

Saturday – SATURN

Midnight		Noon	
SATURN	12 to 1 a.m.	MERCURY	12 to 1 p.m.
JUPITER	1 to 2	MOON	1 to 2
MARS	2 to 3	SATURN	2 to 3
SUN	3 to 4	JUPITER	3 to 4
VENUS	4 to 5	MARS	4 to 5
MERCURY	5 to 6	SUN	5 to 6
MOON	6 to 7	VENUS	6 to 7
SATURN	7 to 8	MERCURY	7 to 8
JUPITER	8 to 9	MOON	8 to 9
MARS	9 to 10	SATURN	9 to 10
SUN	10 to 11	JUPITER	10 to 11
VENUS	11 to 12	MARS	11 to 12

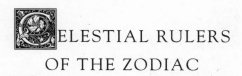ELESTIAL RULERS
OF THE ZODIAC

ANCIENT ASTROLOGY'S enduring gift is the beauty and precision of its celestial patterns. Each zodiac sign had its own element, humour, gender, and planetary ruler. With the exception of the Sun and the Moon, exclusive properties of Leo and Cancer, all the other heavenly mansions were divided into Day and Night abodes:

Aries – Mars, Day, active

Taurus – Venus, Night, passive

Gemini – Mercury, Day, active

Cancer – Moon

Leo – Sun

Virgo – Mercury, Night, passive

Libra – Venus, Day, active

Scorpio – Mars, Night, passive

Sagittarius – Jupiter, Day, active

Capricorn – Saturn, Night, passive

Aquarius – Saturn, Day, active

Pisces – Jupiter, Night, passive

ASTROLOGICAL KEYS

Signs of the Zodiac – *Channels of Expression*

Aries: fiery, pioneering, competitive
Taurus: earthy, stable, practical
Gemini: dual, lively, versatile
Cancer: protective, traditional
Leo: dramatic, flamboyant, warm
Virgo: conscientious, analytical
Libra: refined, fair, sociable
Scorpio: intense, secretive, ambitious
Sagittarius: friendly, expansive
Capricorn: cautious, materialistic
Aquarius: inquisitive, unpredictable
Pisces: responsive, dependent, fanciful

Celestial Bodies – *Generating Energy of the Cosmos*

Sun: birth sign, ego, identity
Moon: emotions, memories, personality
Mercury: communication, intellect, skills
Venus: love, pleasures, the fine arts
Mars: energy, challenges, sports
Jupiter: expansion, religion, happiness
Saturn: responsibility, maturity, realities
Uranus: originality, science, progress
Neptune: dreams, illusions, inspiration
Pluto: rebirth, renewal, resources

Elements

Fire: Aries, Leo, Sagittarius
Earth: Taurus, Virgo, Capricorn
Air: Gemini, Libra, Aquarius
Water: Cancer, Scorpio, Pisces

Qualities

Cardinal	*Fixed*	*Mutable*
Aries	Taurus	Gemini
Cancer	Leo	Virgo
Libra	Scorpio	Sagittarius
Capricorn	Aquarius	Pisces

Cardinal signs mark the beginning of each new season – active. Fixed signs represent the season at its height – steadfast. Mutable signs herald a change of season – variable.

The Houses – *Twelve Areas of Life*

1st house: appearance, image, identity
2nd house: money, possessions, tools
3rd house: communications, siblings
4th house: family, domesticity, security
5th house: romance, creativity, children
6th house: daily routine, service, health
7th house: marriage, partnerships, union
8th house: passion, death, rebirth, soul
9th house: travel, philosophy, education
10th house: fame, achievement, mastery
11th house: goals, friends, high hopes
12th house: sacrifice, solitude, privacy

Glossary of Aspects

Conjunction: two planets within the same sign or less than 10 degrees apart, favorable or unfavorable according to the nature of the planets.

Sextile: a pleasant, harmonious aspect occurring when two planets are two signs or 60 degrees apart.

Square: a major negative effect resulting when planets are three signs from one another or 90 degrees apart.

Trine: planets four signs or 120 degrees apart, forming a positive and favorable influence.

Quincunx: a mildly negative aspect produced when planets are five signs or 150 degrees apart.

Opposition: a six sign or 180 degrees separation of planets generating positive or negative forces depending on the planets involved.

Talismans for the seven days of the week

ELESTIAL GEMS

Venus   *Mercury*

METALS to the seven heavenly bodies of antiquity have remained constant for over two thousand years: the Sun, gold; the Moon, silver; Mars, iron; Mercury, quicksilver; Jupiter, tin; Venus, copper; and Saturn, lead. But the symbolic classification of gems is a difficult and often confusing matter, for the correspondences vary widely from one occult authority to another. By consulting a wide spectrum of sources – ancient, classical, medieval, Renaissance and modern – we've assembled a list of jewels most consistently linked with the Sun, Moon, and particular planets through the centuries of Western occult tradition.

Agate – Mercury ☿
Alexandrite – Mercury ☿
Amber – Moon ☽
Amethyst – Jupiter ♃
Aquamarine – Venus ♀
Beryl – Venus ♀
Bloodstone – Mars ♂
Carbuncle – Venus ♀
Carnelian – Sun ☉
Cat's–eye – Sun ☉
Chalcedony – Saturn ♄
Chrysoprase – Venus ♀
Crystal – Moon ☽
Diamond – Sun ☉
Emerald – Venus ♀
Garnet – Mars ♂
Jacinth – Jupiter ♃

Jade – Venus ♀
Jasper – Mercury ☿
Jet – Saturn ♄
Lapis lazuli – Jupiter ♃
Malachite – Venus ♀
Moonstone – Moon ☽
Onyx – Saturn ♄
Opal – Mercury ☿
Pearl – Moon ☽
Peridot – Venus ♀
Quartz – Moon ☽
Ruby – Mars ♂
Sapphire – Jupiter ♃
Sardonyx – Mercury ☿
Topaz – Sun ☉
Tourmaline – Mercury ☿
Turquoise – Venus ♀

Colonne ardant. Estoille volant.   Comette couee.   Estoilles erratiques.

Les trops dernieres sont estoille barbue estoille cheuelue & estoille couee.

Comet forms

# CHINESE HOROSCOPE

ACCORDING TO ancient astrological lore of the Far East, each year belongs to one of the twelve animals of the zodiac cycle in the following order:

Years of the Rat

1900	1912	1924	1936
1948	1960	1972	1984
1996	2008	2020	2032

Years of the Ox

1901	1913	1925	1937
1949	1961	1973	1985
1997	2009	2021	2033

Years of the Tiger

1902	1914	1926	1938
1950	1962	1974	1986
1998	2010	2022	2034

Years of the Hare

1903	1915	1927	1939
1951	1963	1975	1987
1999	2011	2023	2035

Years of the Dragon

1904	1916	1928	1940
1952	1964	1976	1988
2000	2012	2024	2036

Years of the Snake

1905	1917	1929	1941
1953	1965	1977	1989
2001	2013	2025	2037

Years of the Horse

1906	1918	1930	1942
1954	1966	1978	1990
2002	2014	2026	2038

Years of the Ram

1907	1919	1931	1943
1955	1967	1979	1991
2003	2015	2027	2039

Years of the Monkey

1908	1920	1932	1944
1956	1968	1980	1992
2004	2016	2028	2040

Years of the Cock

1909	1921	1933	1945
1957	1969	1981	1993
2005	2017	2029	2041

Years of the Dog

1910	1922	1934	1946
1958	1970	1982	1994
2006	2018	2030	2042

Years of the Boar

1911	1923	1935	1947
1959	1971	1983	1995
2007	2019	2031	2043

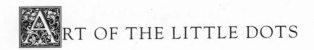

ART OF THE LITTLE DOTS

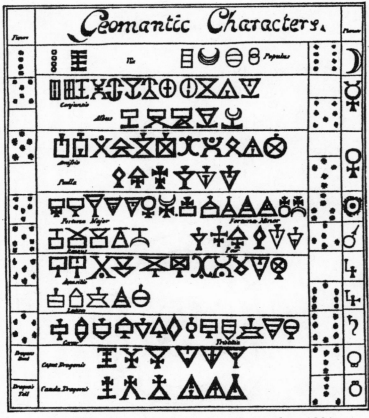

From The Magus by Francis Barrett, London, 1801

GEOMANCY, from the Greek words *geo*, the earth and *manteia*, prophecy, originated centuries ago in the Arab world where the art of sand-divining is still in common practice. Renowned author and magician Cornelius Agrippa introduced geomantic principles to literate Europeans in his *Occult Philosophy*, Volume II, published in Antwerp in 1531. "The Art of the Little Dots," as geomancy was called in 17th-century France, enjoyed a vogue at the court of Louis XIV, where it was regarded as a most reliable oracle. Its answers, then and now, prove provocative, surprising, and more often than not, right on the mark.

The curious fact about geomancy is that it doesn't require sand or earth to be effective. The primary aim is to create a vertical pattern of four rows composed of single and double dots. One dot stands for an odd number. Two dots represent an even number. Classically, the querent makes a random series of holes in the earth with a polished stick. The seer then isolates a certain group and interprets its significance. Another simple and direct method requires only thought, pen, and paper:

Decide on four single digit numbers. You might roll dice, draw playing cards, or just call four to mind as you would for a lottery. Observe one strict rule: concentrate intently on your question while the decision is made. Suppose the numbers you choose are four, two, five, seven.

```
4 - even.        •        •
2 - even.        •        •
5 - odd.             •
7 - odd.             •
```

Match the pattern to one of the sixteen possible combinations and you will find it means *Fortuna Major*, a good-luck portent.

```
        •
        •
        •
        •
```

☽ *Via*, the way. Cultivate patience, for life itself moves slowly in a wandering manner. Bright hope beckons from afar. Expect some detours. Element: Water. Planet: Moon. Sign: Cancer.

```
        •        •
        •        •
        •        •
        •        •
```

☽ *Populus*, reunion with humanity. Understand the crowd, but bend not to popular opinion. Be practical and maintain quiet confidence. Avoid disorder. Element: Water. Planet: Moon. Sign: Cancer.

☿ *Conjunctio*, meeting. Rely on integrated and coordinated effort. Don't lose sight of the primary goal. Proceed in harmony. Communicate to reach concord. Element: Earth. Planet: Mercury. Sign: Virgo.

☿ *Albus*, white, spirituality. Purity of heart and serenity of spirit are your gifts. Protect your home from negative forces. Seek to find a clear horizon. Element: Air. Planet: Mercury. Sign: Gemini.

♀ *Amissio*, loss. Failure and diminution result from passivity. The path of least resistance has many dangers. Take heart and renew your courage. Element: Air. Planet: Venus. Sign: Libra.

♀ *Puella*, femininity, softness. Look for gentleness. Your answer will come in solitude. Escape stress to find true value. Element: Earth. Planet: Venus. Sign: Taurus.

Fortuna major, splendor, good fortune. You've won a victory with honor. Now you must learn to build upon it. Move on. Element: Fire. Planet: Sun. Sign: Leo.

Fortuna minor, success. Worldly success is welcome, not outstanding and not always moral. A time to explore deeper levels of being. Element: Fire. Planet: Sun. Sign: Leo.

♂ *Rubeus*, red, earthiness. Passion overrides good sense. Withdraw until the smoke from the battle clears away. Element: Fire. Planet: Mars. Sign: Aries.

♂ *Puer*, masculinity and solidity. Forthright action is indicated. Take the direct path, but shun violence. Avoid deceit. Element: Fire. Planet: Mars. Sign: Scorpio.

♃ *Acquisitio*, gain. Growth is indicated. Both material and moral success. Beware of taking advantage of those less fortunate. To cheat is to lose. Element: Air. Planet: Jupiter. Sign: Pisces.

♃ *Laetitia*, happiness, joy. A cycle is completed. Wisdom is gained. An end is a beginning. Give praise to those who nurture thee. Element: Air. Planet: Jupiter. Sign: Sagittarius.

♄ *Carcer*, prison, isolation. Free yourself from that which restrains and hinders individual progress. Break the chains of habit. Element: Earth. Planet: Saturn. Sign: Capricorn.

♄ *Tristitia*, misfortune. Restriction and anxiety cloud the question. Review the alternatives. Refuse to accept despair on any terms. Element: Earth. Planet: Saturn. Sign: Aquarius.

∙ ∙
∙
∙
∙

♌ *Caput draconis*, head of the dragon. Peace, inner happiness, fruitfulness will be yours. All pleasures are the products of natural forces. Element: Air. Planet: Moon in ascending node. Sign: Virgo.

∙
∙
∙
∙ ∙

☋ *Cauda draconis*, dragon tail. Outer happiness is threatened by pernicious and destructive forces. Beware of discord. Be alert to possible betrayal. Element: Earth. Planet: Moon in descending node. Sign: Libra.

AROT

THE ANCIENT TAROT is more than a deck of fortune-telling cards. As the precursor of modern playing cards, tarot decks were at one time used as entertainment and for games. Yet the Tarot has always been used for mundane purposes as well as for divination, meditation, spiritual development and magic. The great mysteries are said to be told in the Major Arcana. The series of 22 images that make up the Major Arcana have also been linked to the journey of the Fool and the path taken by initiates following initiation. During the divination process, known as cartomancy, the deck is shuffled and the mingling of the seeker's personal energies with the powerful images on the cards causes the unfolding of events to be mimicked in the spread of the cards. This spread is interpreted by the reader and the hidden becomes revealed. One way to use the individual cards as charms would be to choose the appropriate card and place it on or near the object or person to be influenced. A woman wishing to conceive would carry the Empress card. An athlete wishing to win a race could place the Chariot card in his footwear. When performing a curse, the Tower card becomes invaluable. Let the card associations become a guide to your meditations or for use in making a charm.

0   **The Fool** – an important choice.

1   **The Magician** – the ability to direct power, oneness or unity, skill, negotiation, to make manifest.

2   **The High Priestess** – mystery, the unknown, what is hidden, calm, duality, silence.

3   **The Empress** – fertility, marriage, growth, creative arts, wealth, inspiration.

4   **The Emperor** – leadership, guidance, power, intelligence over passion, authority, command.

5   **The Hierophant** – convention, conformity, approval, rules and regulation, control, tradition, habit.

6   **The Lovers** – choice, harmony, attraction, beauty, magnetism, splendor, accord.

7   **The Chariot** – movement, triumph, achievement, travel, artistic endeavors, conquest, attainment.

8   **Strength** – triumph of higher over lower desires.

9   **The Hermit** – spiritual wisdom, attainment, guidance, prudence, council, advice, caution, care.

10 **The Wheel of Fortune** – turn for the better, increased luck, good fortune, success, triumph.

11 **Justice** – favorable outcome in legal matters.

12 **The Hanged Man** – delay, surrendering to another cause, a change in life.

13 **Death** – change, transformation, death, reincarnation.

14 **Temperance** – balance, good judgment, adaptation, modification, consolation, alteration.

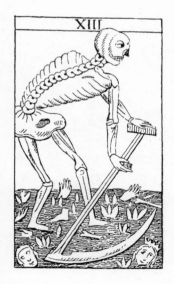

15 The Devil – material bondage, force, sickness, stagnation.

16 The Tower – catastrophe, overthrow of what currently exists, upset, bankruptcy, demise.

17 The Star – hope, inspiration, the spiritual, health, light is in sight, bravery, insight.

18 The Moon – deception, secrets, imagination, dark creativity, intuition, dreams, the unconscious.

19 The Sun – attainment, success, happiness, achievements, liberation, pleasures, joy.

20 **Judgment** – an overdue change, an awakening, arousing.

21 **The World** – success, completion, achievement, reward, victory, conquest.

GLOSSARY

Adept: A skilled practitioner of the occult arts.

Alchemy: Medieval science dedicated to turning base metals into gold.

Amulet: A charm worn to avert evil and attract good luck.

Aradia: The legendary daughter of deities Diana and Lucifer, destined to teach witchcraft to mortals.

Arcane: Descriptive word meaning secret knowledge of the ancients.

Archetype: The original model or pattern.

Astral Body: Spirit body.

Atavism: Of or pertaining to a remote ancestor in instinctive memory.

Athame: Black-hilted knife used in the rites of a ceremonial magician.

Augury: Divination.

Aura: A halo or emanation of light surrounding an individual.

Avalon: The Celtic abode of the blessed; paradise of Arthurian legend.

Balefire: A great fire blazing in the open air; a bonfire.

Bane: That which destroys life.

Banshee: Gaelic spirit whose wail warns of pproaching death.

Bard: Celtic poet; a singer of tales.

Beltane: Celtic name for the festival celebrated on May Eve.

Blocula: An Elfdale county estate where Swedish witches attended the sabbat festivals.

Bloodstone: A green gem sprinkled with red spots; the heliotrope of magic.

Book of Shadows: A collection of ancient rituals, chants, spells and enchantments copied down in the handwriting of a witch.

Bride: Brigit, Bridget, or Brid is the pre-Celtic goddess of Ireland symbolizing the promise of spring.

Brocken: The highest peak in the Hartz mountains of northern Germany known as a gathering place for witches.

By Kynde: By nature, or instinct.

Cabala: Hebraic system of mystical thought; an esoteric doctrine of urban medieval society.

Cairn: A Gaelic term for a stone pile that accumulates when a field is cleared for planting.

Candlemas: A festival of light observed on the eve of February 2. Also the Feast of Bride that celebrates the coming of spring.

Chalice: A silver cup used in sacred ceremonies of witchcraft.

Changeling: A child secretly exchanged for another in infancy.

Cone of Power: The collected force of powerful wills focused on a single purpose.

Coven: A group of witches working to achieve a common purpose.

Cult: A shared system of belief or worship.

Cunning Man: Known in Elizabethan England as one thought able to combat the will of witches.

Deasil: To move sunwise or clockwise, from left to right. A charm performed by going three times around an object carrying fire in the right hand.

Déjà Vu: Fleeting personal memory of a previous life.

Demeter: Greek goddess of the earth; known to the Romans as Ceres.

Diana: Roman goddess of the Moon and the hunt; called Artemis by the Greeks.

Dionysian Mysteries: Rites of worship celebrated to honor the god of the vine and earth.

Dirae: Omen.

Druid: One of the priestly class of Celtic culture. A modern follower of ancient ways.

Dualism: A philosophical concept of opposing principles which form the ultimate nature of the universe as, for example, good and evil.

Dyad: Two units; a pair.

Eleusinian Mysteries: Rites dedicated to the worship of Demeter and Persephone.

Equinox: The time when day and night are of equal length.

Esbat: Weekly meeting of witches.

Evil Eye: A baleful glance capable of causing harm.

Exorcism: A Christian ritual practiced to expel evil spirits.

Familiar: Animal helper of a witch in casting enchantments and working spells.

Fetch: Apparition.

Fetish: An object possessing magic power derived from the spirit dwelling within it.

Freya: Nordic goddess of love for whom Friday is named.

Gnosticism: The system of philosophy and religion which asserts mankind may possess inner knowledge by direct revelation.

Grimoire: A text of magical rites and spells.

Hallowmas: November Eve festival of witchcraft.

Hecate: Patroness of witchcraft; a triple goddess of the Moon, Earth, and Underworld.

Herodias: Goddess of witches; Diana as Queen of the Night.

Hex: A spell or a charm, derived from the German word for witchcraft.

Hierophant: High priest of the Eleusinian mysteries.

Hubris: Man's exasperation with fate and life's limitations.

I Ching: Chinese Book of Changes; collected wisdom of ancient origin.

Incantation: Chant spoken slowly with firm intent.

Janus: Double-faced Roman god who watched both the rising and setting Sun.

La Tene: The Iron Age in Europe, dating from 800 B.C.E. to C.E. 100.

Lammas: Festival of witchcraft held on August Eve to insure good harvest.

Ligature: A binding.

Loki: Nordic god of fire.

Lughnassad: Celtic name for the August Eve celebration.

Macrocosm / Microcosm: The universe as contrasted to man; what is equal above, is equal below.

Magus: Wise man.

Need-Fire: A flame produced by friction in ceremony used to ignite the bonfires of May Eve.

Odin: Nordic god of wisdom and poetry. Also called Woden.

Oimelc: Celtic name for the celebration held on the eve of February 2.

Overlook: To cast a glance of power for good or ill.

Owl Time: Between midnight and one o'clock; the 13th hour.

Pentacle: Five-pointed star, an ancient symbol of perfection used from the time of Pythagoras, Greek philosopher and mathematician, 6th century B.C.E.

Persephone: The daughter of Demeter / Ceres who was abducted by the god of the underworld. Her return each year symbolizes springtime. The Romans called her Proserpine.

Philtre: A potion prepared to produce a magical effect, especially a love charm.

Psyche: The human soul, the mind, the inner thought.

Rites of Passage: Human transitions celebrated at birth, puberty, marriage and death.

Runes: Germanic alphabet derived in large measure from the Greek and Roman; formed with straight lines to facilitate carving on stone and wood.

Sabbat: Feast. Major sabbats are November Eve, February1, May Eve, and August Eve. The lesser sabbats are celebrated at winter and summer solstices; spring (vernal) and fall (autumnal) equinoxes.

Samhain: The Celtic name for the sacred November Eve celebration; Hallowmas.

Satanism: Christian devil worship; an inversion or parody of Christian faith.

Scry: To divine by means of crystal ball, mirror or other reflective surface.

Shaman: Sorcerer of primitive tribes. A medium between the visible and the spirit world.

Signatures, Doctrine of: The belief that each plant bears a visible key to its use.

Solitary: One who practices the art of witchcraft alone.

Solstice: The longest day of the year, Midsummer Day, June 21; the shortest day, December 21, when the Sun begins its return and the days lengthen.

Sooth: Truth.

Swan-road: The sea.

Talisman: An object marked under certain conditions of the heavens to act as a charm against evil.

Traditionals: A term used to designate members of the witch-cult who practice rites handed down through the generations; hereditary witches.

Vates: Prophets.

Walpurgisnacht: Germanic name for the May Eve festival.

Watchers: The sleepless ones or "fallen angels" of Hebrew legend who mated with the daughters of men to whom they taught the forbidden arts.

Warlock: An Anglo-Saxon term of derision, i.e., a liar and betrayer of trust.

Widdershins: Backward, or in a direction contrary to the apparent motion of the Sun. To move counter-clockwise.

Witch Balls: Spheres of colored glass intended to thwart evil spirits and protect the home.

Wort: Any plant or herb.

Wyrd: Anglo-Saxon goddess of destiny.

Yule: Norse feast celebrating winter solstice.

Zoroaster: Prophet who flourished in Persia about 1000 B.C.E.

Other fine books from The Witches' Almanac Ltd.

The Horned Shepherd

Greek Gods in Love

Witches All

Magical Creatures

Love Charms

Ancient Roman Holidays

Celtic Tree Magic

Moon Lore

Magic Spells and Incantations

Love Feasts

Random Recollections

The Witches' Almanac

Order online at www.TheWitchesAlmanac.com